THE STRANGER AT EMMAUS

THE STRANGER AT EMMAUS

And Other New Testament Stories

BY BOB GOSSETT

Copyright © 1972
Herald Publishing House
Independence, Missouri

All rights in this book are reserved. No part of the text may be reproduced in any form without written permission of the publishers, except brief quotations used in connection with reviews in magazines or newspapers.

Library of Congress
Catalog Card No. 72-83275

ISBN-0-8309-0076-4

Printed in the United States of America

Contents

The Stranger at Emmaus 7

Madness in the Tombs 17

A Touch of Faith 25

Sight at Siloam 33

Lazarus: Profile of Resurrection 43

The Ear of Malchus 51

Interrupted Funeral 59

Angel of Deliverance 63

Black Magic and Blue Tapestry 77

Pagan Nightmare 87

The Stranger at Emmaus

Based on Luke 24:13-35

Cleopas had made up his mind. He would venture outside and go about his business just as though nothing had happened. His decision to become involved again in the everyday affairs of a Jerusalem businessman would not seem to be so difficult to make were it not for certain momentous events which had occurred in the city within the past three days.

For one thing, all his friends were now in hiding. They had been associated with a fanatical religious group led by a young Jew by the name of Jesus from the town of Nazareth. This Jew had met his death by crucifixion just seventy-two hours earlier. It had never been made quite clear by the authorities why he had been arrested and put to death nor what his crime had been.

There were some within the city who had formerly opposed the work of the young prophet and healer who now declared—though not publicly—that perhaps he had been the victim of a gross miscarriage of Roman justice. Cleopas had to smile wryly at this thought. It seemed so tragically ironic that the very God of love and justice whom Jesus had proclaimed so convincingly had now allowed him to suffer the extreme penalty—and for no real cause.

For the majority of the populace the very idea of the claim of Jesus to be the Son of God had been a colossal farce from start to finish, or at best a tragic illusion. Cleopas could not bring himself to accept the fact that it was all over now. Yet, there was the wreckage of the simple faith that Jesus had preached, strewn about for all to behold. For one thing the Master had told them, "There is no man that hath left house, or parents or brethren or wife or children, for the kingdom of God's sake, who shall not receive manifold more in this present time, and in the world to come, life everlasting." Cleopas knew of two business acquaintances who had left their homes and their livelihoods to follow Jesus. They had not only lost their businesses but their wives and families had deserted them in their folly. They were now outcasts, hiding as best they could, as he himself had been doing for the past several days.

There was the man Matthew who had had a good position with the Roman occupational government, collecting taxes for Caesar. One day he had left his place of business to go after this dreamer, and he too was without a place to lay his head. Danger was on all sides for any suspected of having given allegiance or assistance to the carpenter from Nazareth. Those few who were still possessed of homes were forced to keep their doors and windows locked at all hours. Even Simon Peter the fisherman now found it almost impossible to market his catches in the ancient city.

Truly it seemed that the bubble had burst and reality was staring them full in the face. They were despised and shunned even more than the lepers who frequented the city. Nevertheless, Cleopas had made his decision. No longer would he torture himself with thoughts of what the people might think of him or what they might do to him. He would quit the solitude of his home and venture abroad among his fellow citizens. After all, was he not also a taxpayer to the Romans?

Did he not have a perfect right to be upon a public street?

He was considering the idea of walking over to the home of Andrew to talk with him for a while. No sooner had he stepped out into the narrow cobblestone street that led down to the marketplace than two small boys approached him.

One of them recognized him and promptly picked up a paving stone with the clear intent to heave it in the direction of Cleopas.

"That's old Cleopas!" he shouted to the younger boy. "My mother told me she talked to Simon Peter the night of the big crucifixion and she said Peter lied and said he never knew Jesus. Cleopas is Peter's friend and he is a liar just like Peter!" His shouting was punctuated by the resounding crunch of the flagstone as it smashed into the wall directly behind Cleopas. A crowd had begun to gather now. Cleopas ducked into the safety of an alleyway and hurried on toward the home of Andrew, Simon Peter's brother.

Cleopas knocked and knocked and at length the door opened slowly. "Andrew, it is I, Cleopas!" he whispered in a husky tone. Quickly the door closed behind him and the street was quiet except for the lone barking of a stray dog somewhere near the public fountain.

Andrew was somewhat younger than Cleopas, and unmarried. He kept most of his fishing equipment inside the house now. Much of it was piled in disorderly array in one corner of the small room to prevent theft and further damage to his belongings. His small fishing boat, which he had brought up to the house from the beach for repairs, had sustained gaping holes in the sides and bottom. Several nets, hung out to dry in the sunshine, were now slashed beyond repair.

"Cleopas! Why have you dared to leave your home while it is yet day?" gasped the younger man as he bolted the heavy door. He was understandably concerned for their safety. Threats were flying in the city, and not one of the former band of disciples was safe from the fury of the townspeople.

Andrew's tone shifted to one of hope. "Cleopas, have you news?" he said, half afraid to believe that any good thing could happen anymore.

"No, Andrew, no news," Cleopas spoke softly. "Mine is merely a mission of selfishness, I'm afraid. I could no longer endure the loneliness of that dark and cheerless house of mine; I've come to ask you to accompany me to Emmaus."

"What?" exclaimed Andrew, almost shouting. "Do you want to expose us to certain death? Don't you know what is in store for us out there if the mood of the city changes very much more? It would be madness to tempt them any further."

"Yes," replied Cleopas, laying his hand firmly on Andrew's arm. "I am aware of our danger. But, Andrew, people forget. Perhaps their anger has cooled a little. It's been three days now. I would like to inquire of some of my friends in Emmaus about the prospects for business in that village. I may decide to leave Jerusalem until this trouble is forgotten."

After some moments of reflection Andrew replied slowly, "Perhaps that is what we should do, after all. First, let us have something to eat, and then we will go to Emmaus."

. . . . .

The exit of the two from the northwest sector of the city was scarcely noticed. The day was fast drawing to a close and people were making preparations to retire to their homes. Shops were closing and the marketplace now contained only a few late shoppers. Smoke curled lazily against the fading light of the Jerusalem sky as evening meals were being prepared, and life moved on much as it had always done in the ancient walled city.

Two elderly women, one of whom carried a wicker basket filled with fruits, passed Andrew and Cleopas in the near-deserted street. Recognition lit their eyes as they approached the men, turning instantly to frowns of disgust as Andrew spoke a word of greeting.

"I suppose we will have to become accustomed to that, Andrew, if we stay in Jerusalem," said Cleopas.

"That, or something worse!" mused the younger man.

The seven-mile journey to Emmaus had been an event toward which Cleopas, as a small boy, had looked forward as he had accompanied his father to that village on business. This evening, however, there was no anticipation of pleasure—nothing to look forward to, no happiness to be shared, nothing. It was simply a trip to be endured, a change of scenery.

The coolness of the late afternoon was a welcome change from the drab surroundings and the stale air to which they had become accustomed in the city for the past three days.

A spirit of melancholy gripped the hearts of Cleopas and Andrew as they traveled the familiar old road once again. In a happier time Jesus and his band of disciples had traversed this very road speaking of heavenly things, impossible dreams. Now there remained only descending degrees of despair as they walked slowly along, each alone with his thoughts.

Andrew broke the silence. "Cleopas, I had trusted so strongly that Jesus was truly the Son of God. I believed it with all my heart. How could he have been so convincing if he were not Messiah? Did he not perform miracles and did he not speak as no other has ever spoken?" Andrew kicked up a flurry of dust with his sandal in a gesture of helpless rage. He continued in a voice choked with emotion. "His idea of the kingdom of God was such a wonderful illusion. But I loved him, dreams and all. For some strange, compelling reason I loved him, though I hid like a coward during his trial and crucifixion. I am so bewildered and crushed in my heart, Cleopas." Andrew ended with a swipe of his hand across his eye, and tried hard to pretend it was but a cinder.

"Andrew," began Cleopas, "we all loved him—all, I suppose, except Judas. There was something about him that drew a man to him and brought out the best in him, in spite of himself. I suppose," continued Cleopas, "that this is the way all such things have to end. Men seem determined to have none of God and prefer to go their own way. Have they not stones enough to kill all the prophets sent to them?" Cleopas adjusted the shoulder strap of the traveling bag he carried and looked anxiously in the direction of Emmaus.

The sun was surrendering to the first gray streaks of evening and there was a redness in the western sky that cast a pale pinkish glow over the entire countryside. As the two men rounded a bend, they made out the figure of a man standing in the road who seemed to be waiting for them. They quickened their step; they did not relish the idea of having to battle their way out of an ambush. Road bandits were common around Jerusalem, and a traveler might encounter several before he had gone very far from Jerusalem's protective walls. The lone figure was soon within hailing distance.

"Friends," he began, "if you are going toward Emmaus, would you mind if I accompanied you? It is far safer to be with others when on the road."

"Certainly, friend. Join us," responded Cleopas as Andrew glanced furtively about.

The stranger carried himself with dignity and in no way resembled the highwaymen who frequented the roads leading out of Jerusalem. His hair was dark and he wore a short beard typical of the young men of the day. His eyes seemed to pierce the inward recesses of the heart as he gazed upon the two men from the troubled city. He was young, physically strong, yet his presence seemed vested with an otherworldliness.

It was difficult for Andrew to shape an opinion of this man. There was the haunting feeling that he was one whom they had known somewhere in the past.

"I saw you two talking so earnestly as you walked along the road. You seemed to be discussing something very important—and very sad—from the appearance of your faces. What could engage your attention so?" queried the stranger.

Cleopas replied almost with rudeness, "Could it be that you are the only man around Jerusalem who has not heard what has been going on back there for the past few days?"

"Perhaps. But suppose you tell me. What things?" asked the traveler.

The last rays of the setting sun rested on the group as they walked toward Emmaus. The stranger lifted his hand to wipe his brow, and Andrew thought for a fleeting second that he detected an ugly red scar in the palm. His emotions leaped within him in spite of himself, but he told himself firmly that he had had quite enough of disillusionment.

Cleopas continued to relate the events that had transpired in Jerusalem. His tale revolved about the person of a young prophet named Jesus whom some had referred to as the Messiah. He had been the one upon whom the people had set their hopes for deliverance from Roman tyranny. Cleopas told of the brief ministry of this strange man who called himself the Son of Man. He told how Jesus had established his church and of his untimely death and their own dashed hopes.

The attitude of the stranger was one of courteous attention. Abruptly, he asked, "This man Jesus. What became of him after his death? Did his friends bury him properly? I understand it is the Roman custom in criminal executions to remove the body from the cross, dump it in the garbage heaps, and deny burial."

Cleopas was quick to answer. "No! Oh, no! We loved him. One of our wealthy men requested the body and was given permission to bury it in the tomb he had purchased for himself. Strangely, though, some of our women told us that they went to the sepulcher just this morning at an early hour, and his body was missing. It is said they saw a vision of angels at the tomb who told them that Jesus was not there, that he had risen from the dead. Can you imagine our surprise? At any rate, several men went to the tomb also and they were not able to locate the body anywhere. Now we do not even have so much as a grave to remind us of him whom we loved."

Suddenly the stranger spoke as though he knew more of the significance of these things than the disciples themselves. "Oh, how foolish you are," he chided, "not to believe the prophecies concerning the Messiah and his work. He suffered because it was part of the plan of the Father for the redemption not only of Israel but of all mankind." He then began to reveal to them the meaning of the Scriptures, beginning with the books of Moses and relating prophecies to the crucified carpenter.

Still the sorrow of the loss of their beloved young leader did not lift, and the two disciples could not perceive who it was that talked with them in so gracious a manner.

Presently, the village of Emmaus lay before them. It was now quite dark, and the men from Jerusalem began formulating plans for an overnight stay in one of the inns there. As they entered the outlying district where the camel drivers stabled their beasts and secured lodging for themselves for a night, they saw a familiar inn and made their way toward it.

The stranger bade them farewell and turned as though to continue his journey. Something caused the two to constrain their friend and to entreat him to stay the night with them. Their spirits had been lifted as they had listened to his optimistic counsel concerning their crucified teacher.

Graciously the stranger accepted their invitation, and the three entered the inn together.

Cleopas brought out bread and dried meat and a wineskin from the bag he had carried from Jerusalem and the men sat down to the evening meal. It was the strange friend from the roadside who offered thanks for a safe journey and for the food of which they were about to partake.

Surely they could not have dreamed what happened next, for it occurred with lightning speed. Suddenly they beheld, in the place of a stranger at the table, something of the effulgence of heaven itself. The entire room was aglow as with the brilliance from a million candles. In the midst of this dazzling brightness sat the living Christ!

Utterly dumbfounded, the disciples sat in open-mouthed astonishment at the glory before them.

"Lord, do we dream or is it really thee?" gasped Cleopas.

With a soft, "Fear not; it is I," Jesus vanished from their sight.

Unrestrained joy and wonder flooded the hearts of Andrew and Cleopas as they realized that theirs was not a lost cause; theirs was not a dead and buried leader. Theirs was, indeed, the ultimate and triumphant victory of life over death. Their Christ was truly alive!

Cleopas gazed into the brimming eyes of the younger man, grasped his arm, and said in even tones, "Did you not have the feeling of a fire burning in your heart as he talked with us on the road and opened the Scriptures to us?"

Andrew could only nod his head and smile through a flood of hot tears that trickled into his beard.

As they reached the road which led into Jerusalem, the night was no longer dark.

Madness in the Tombs

Based on Mark 5:1-15

The villagers were right to drive him out. Perhaps he was possessed, after all. Maybe it was actually a demon that had caused his behavior. There could be no returning home now. Not after what he had done.

Mithridates, a young man from the Greek village of Gadara, sat on a great rock that overlooked the sea and tried to sort his thinking.

It had not been the first time that this had happened to him. Several other days were forever obliterated from his mind, gone with the madness that had seized upon him and caused him untold anguish and misery. Once, he knew, he had almost caused the death of a child, in a frenzied moment lost somewhere in the dim recesses of his memory.

It had happened with the furious swiftness of a cyclonic wind, blowing out the flame of intelligence and reason within his brain. One moment he was talking with some friends from one of the neighboring cities of the Decapolis; the next, he was the personification of evil as he slashed at the people about him and screamed like a spirit from the abode of the damned. Without warning, his whole world had exploded before him. Having gained a reputation among the townspeople as a philosopher of some note, it had been his delight to discuss with other inquiring minds the ideas of the great thinkers of the ages. All had come to regard the young

Mithridates as a man of great promise and gave rapt attention when he spoke in the public forum.

On that day, as he sat on the stone steps of the great Fountain House that commanded the road leading to the Acropolis, he argued as usual with his good friends the finer points of the philosophies of Socrates and Plato.

Without warning, a deadening pain swelled through his temples, almost blinding him. He could remember the startled look on the face of his dear friend Apelles as he beheld the change that came over the youthful philosopher. A surge of madness seemed to settle over his mind like a shroud. Leaping to his feet, Mithridates seized the terrified Apelles by his tunic, jerking him to his full height and smashing his fist hard into the face of his friend.

Turning, Mithridates saw the citizens on the steps rise and begin to move away from him. He remembered the fear that had filled their eyes as they watched him. Screaming in agony, he ran down the steps, tearing his cape from about his shoulders. Dashing into the street, he was nearly run down by an oxcart laden with great earthen jars, making its way to the nearby market. He suddenly seized a small child from its mother's arms and ran back toward the cart, whose owner now sat staring at the crazed young man.

Lifting the child above his head, he was about to cast it headlong at the feet of the oxen which had come to a halt in the middle of the street. Something caused him to pause, child screaming in midair. A look of bewilderment crossed his face as he lowered the child and looked at it, cradled in his arms, as though he was uncertain as to how it came to be there. Gently, he set the baby on the ground, and as its mother rushed forward from the crowd, Mithridates looked blankly at the great number of people who stood helplessly by.

Apelles, a streak of blood running from the corner of his

mouth, crossed the square, took Mithridates gently by the arm, and led him toward the stoa which stood impressively in the center of the town, facing east. This was the great public portico supported on four sides by a massive colonnade and dedicated to Zeus, father of the gods.

Visibly shaken, Mithridates wept openly as Apelles attempted in vain to comfort his friend. As the two sat on the steps of the great meeting place, beneath a marble relief of Zeus and Apollo, they heard the footsteps of many people ascending the stoa. Looking up, Apelles saw a group of men advancing toward them led by an ephor, or chief justice of the city. Mithridates bolted upright as the citizens approached him. He recoiled in abject fear as the ephor stepped closer and read from a scroll which stated that Mithridates had endangered the lives and welfare of the citizens of Gadara for the last time. From time to time, the ephor cast nervous glances at Mithridates, whose disposition was apt to change momentarily. Proceeding further in the proclamation, the ephor noted that it had been drawn up at the behest of concerned citizens and submitted to the ekklesia, or citizens assembly, for action.

After the delegation left the stoa, Mithridates stood looking at his friend. He put an arm about Apelles and smiled knowingly.

With emotion choking his voice, Apelles said, "This does not mean that you are forever banished from among us, nor that you can never return to Gadara."

"No, my friend, I shall never again be a burden to the good citizens of this city," said Mithridates.

"But where will you go, what will you do?"

"Somewhere beyond the habitation of man I shall make my dwelling place. I am not well, Apelles, I know that. These good people should not have to endure madness among them. My agony shall not be their agony; I will leave."

As Mithridates started to leave the great porch, Apelles walked with him to the steps and said, "May the gods be with you, my dear friend. Remember this, your friends are still your friends, and we shall be here when you find yourself and come back to us."

Mithridates, his mind already in turmoil again, walked slowly down the long flight of marble steps, turned, and lifted his hand in a farewell to Apelles and his broken past.

. . . . .

It was with no little foreboding that Mithridates had made his way toward the forbidden burial area, south of the city, toward the sea. This was the abandoned place of burial, long since fallen into decay and neglect, which had been used to bury the fallen of the Battle of Salamis. It was only after this noteworthy battle that Athens had become a great naval power, having destroyed half the Persian fleet. Legend held that the disembodied spirits of the dead lurked within the tombs, awaiting the arrival of an unfortunate mortal who might happen that way, whose fate would be unspeakable.

Mithridates pulled himself from his reverie and stood looking out over the sea. His mind was clear now, and he felt no pain from the ugly scars that laced his arms. Since his arrival at the seacoast three days earlier, he had suffered immeasurable anguish. The times he had become helplessly embroiled in a spell of mental agony in Gadara had proved to be merely a preface to the torture he must now endure. The rocky, jagged hills had echoed with the unearthly screams of the possessed Mithridates, who beat his chest and lacerated his arms and face with the sharp stones which lay along the shore. His piercing wail could be heard reverberating among the sea cliffs which guarded the ancient tombs that dotted the hillside toward the sea.

Travelers judiciously avoided this area, as popular belief contended that danger from the other world was ever present there. Should one be so unfortunate as to pass that way, he must do so in absolute silence for fear of attracting the fury of the spirits that dwelt among the shadows.

Perhaps the men who came from Gadara on the second night of Mithridates' stay in the tombs had in mind to sacrifice this demon-possessed mortal to the spirits of the dead. They had come in strength, some carrying chains and some holding long whips and nets. Perhaps their intention was to offer Mithridates to the restless dead in an effort to appease them and thus make their city safe. For whatever reason, they had come, and they had made the state of the tormented young man more miserable than ever. It had been a murderous encounter. When finally the mad philosopher had been overpowered and chained securely, three Gadarenes lay motionless in the pale cast of the cloudy moon, throats ripped and eyes staring into the black sky.

Reason had completely forsaken Mithridates as he thrashed about attempting to shake himself free of the bonds. His back oozed red in the moonglow, gory token of the slash of the whip. He wept aloud and the wail of pain lifted on the night air and carried among the echoing cliffs of the sea. He staggered now beneath the weight of the chains and the numberless stripes of swollen flesh over his body. He stumbled toward the edge of the sea, falling and regaining his feet, as he made for the coolness of the water. Reaching the edge of the pounding surf, he collapsed headlong into the watery darkness, letting the water move slowly over the stinging wounds.

Refreshed, his face streaming, he shook his head and looked up at the sky. With a mighty effort, he stumbled to his feet, standing ankle-deep in the sea, and glared upward into the blackness of the night. The pale moonlight etched the features of his tormented face as he swept the sky with bloodshot eyes, as though he would invoke the aid of the gods. He lifted the arm that was not strapped to his side by chains and held it pleadingly toward the sky. He stood in that stance until the arm began to grow numb. Dropping his arm to his side, he began to flex his shoulder muscles beneath the cold chains. With a tremendous burst of power, born of the madness that raged within him, the tormented Gadarene snapped the steel links that bound him. Grasping some of the chains that had not fallen to the water, he dashed them against the rocks, howling with rage and pain.

. . . . .

The rugged cliffs of Gadara loomed before the small ship in which the much publicized Jesus of Nazareth sat.

"Master, the Greek colony of Gadara is before us now," said Peter, adjusting the sails as the ship neared the shoals.

"The Greeks will not receive us well," mused Andrew, "for they have their gods and their philosophy, which does not include the God of Israel."

"Nevertheless," replied Jesus, "the Father has given me commandment, and I must work the works of him who sent me, while it is day."

By now, the ship had approached a place along the shore which was free of shoals and treacherous undercurrents, and the disciples made fast the line and prepared to disembark.

The hillside, punctuated by countless tombs, towered before them as they walked along the beach. Presently, Jesus gave the command to ascend the steep embankment which led to the forbidden burial grounds above.

As the foreboding spectacle of the sepulchers loomed before them, the disciples edged nearer to the Master.

Though it was daytime, this area still appeared forbidding and desolate.

Suddenly, out from among the tombs rushed the frenzied Mithridates, eyes wide and glowering, screaming at the top of his voice. It was as though the fury of hell itself had been unleashed as the madman rushed at them, stopping short before the commanding figure of the Christ. Tearing at himself, Mithridates screamed, "I know you! You're Jesus, the Son of God! You have come to torment me! Leave me, leave me, please have mercy and torment me not!"

With great sobs racking his frame, Mithridates dropped to his knees before Jesus. He placed his hands over his ears and screamed, "I can hear them! I can hear them! They won't leave me alone! Go away so they will leave me alone . . . please!"

He swayed there in front of the Master, moaning and holding his ears. With infinite tenderness, Jesus reached out and placed a hand on the Gadarene's shoulder.

"What is your name?" he asked firmly.

"My name . . . my name . . . is Legion. Legion! Legion! Legion!" Mithridates screamed, still holding his head.

The chilly air of the morning was beginning to affect the unclothed body of the demoniac. He shivered in the shifting mists, continuing to babble incoherently.

Jesus looked at John and said simply, "Bring forth a cloak for him."

John took his cloak which draped the length of his vesture and placed it gently over the shuddering Mithridates. Strangely, a look of appreciation lit his eyes as he looked up at the disciple. Then another seizure transformed his face in a flush of furious anger. Suddenly he arose, reaching for the throat of Jesus. He never completed the thrust; an unseen power emanated from the presence of the Master, and

Mithridates was unable to move. He stood weeping, his hands still outstretched toward the Christ.

Jesus placed his hand on the head of the Gadarene and spoke with authority, "I command you, come out of him!"

Obediently, the quivering body of Mithridates ceased its spasms. He lowered his arms as the light of sanity returned to his eyes. A look of deep peace replaced the terrible distortions of mental agony that had been his.

The stillness was split by a shrill squeal, prolonged and unearthly. The cliffs resounded with a chorus of ear-splitting screams from something not human.

One of the disciples pointed beyond the tomb area toward a small pasture on the side of the hill where they stood. There, rushing headlong to the dizzy precipice and hurling themselves into the churning water below, was a vast herd of swine. Their screams echoed through the hills as they rushed over one another in their dash for the edge of the cliff.

Silence followed as the last animal flung itself into the foaming water hundreds of feet below. Stunned, the keepers of the swine walked dazedly to the brow of the hill and looked at the destruction upon the jagged rocks of the shore. Then they turned and fled, for well they knew the legends of the ancient tombs and they feared for their lives as they sprinted to the safety of Gadara.

The disciples, engrossed in watching the swine plunge into the sea, had forgotten for the moment the more tremendous drama being enacted before them. They now beheld Mithridates, formerly the madman of the tombs, seated at the feet of Jesus, John's cloak wrapped about him, and in his right mind. Once more the young philosopher could argue the finer points of the wisdom of the ancients, but now he could speak with personal knowledge of the power of Jesus Christ.

A Touch of Faith

Based on Mark 5:21-43

Situated on the heights above the city of Capernaum stood the synagogue, its white limestone walls catching the faint morning light. Rectangular and facing to the north, it was designed by Jewish law to be entered by means of any one of three doors from a platform on the south. An open court ran the length of the east side of the structure. It was here that devout Jews prepared themselves for entrance into the sacred building. Here, too, in the strategically important city of Capernaum Jesus had performed many of his early miracles and had summoned to his service Peter, Andrew, and Matthew.

The Romans had early seen the advantage of utilizing the location of this town as an administrative center and garrison outpost. Quartered in Capernaum were many of the Emperor's elite assault troops. Military maneuvers included the use of pontoon boats which supported a crude bridge across the Sea of Galilee, the small craft floating gently upon the blue waters. Several companies of crimson-cloaked Roman soldiers were crossing over to the far side for participation in a parade to be held later in the day.

In a darkened quarter of the synagogue, reserved for the special use of the priest, a lone figure knelt before the lighted candles on the altar.

Jairus, a ruler of the synagogue, was a devoted priest and

a scholar of some note. He knelt in the darkness now, brow furrowed with lines which bespoke sleepless nights and constant vigil and the concern familiar only to those who love deeply. The object of his fervent prayers was his only child, a frail daughter who had been beset with various ailments from the day of her birth.

Jairus had come to the synagogue one last time to implore the God of Israel for the life of his daughter. His lips moved slightly as he intoned a priestly supplication in her behalf. Many had been the times that Jairus had knelt here to intercede for the people of Capernaum. Now his earnest prayer was solely for the life of his own dear one who lay at the point of death at his home a few yards away. His cheeks glistened with the moisture of hot tears.

A door opened quietly at the rear of the sanctuary, admitting a young rabbi who moved quickly down the aisle of the sanctuary and stopped beside the kneeling figure.

"Forgive me, but I must tell you the news," he began excitedly.

"My daughter is dead. Isn't that your message?" Jairus replied quietly.

"She is still very ill, but I bring news of the arrival of the man called Jesus, from Nazareth. He only a few moments ago entered Capernaum from the sea. He is at the shore even now with his disciples, teaching and healing many of the sick. I myself saw a leper cleansed before my very eyes, and a crippled child was made to walk. Surely this man is of God."

Jairus rose and started for the door which led to the covered porch.

"I have heard many things of this man. Perhaps he can do something for my child. I must try to see him face to face." Jairus opened the great door and stepped out into the light of the new day.

Following the main road which led down to the seaside,

Jairus and the rabbi walked rapidly until they saw a great throng of people clustered about a small ship at a mooring place on the sandy beach.

Edging their way through the crowd of people listening intently to the man called Christ, they could hear the authoritative tone of Jesus as he taught concerning the kingdom of God. Jairus watched in fascination as a man was carried to a place on the ground before Jesus. The man was familiar to Jairus, a crippled beggar whose entire lifetime had been spent in a bed which was carried by friends from place to place. He gazed in wonder as the wasted and twisted legs of the beggar were gently removed from beneath the dirty blanket by one of the disciples. Without so much as touching the man, Jesus spoke the words of release as he looked on the wretched man lying in the sand. Jairus thrilled when he heard the command of Christ, "I say unto you, arise, take up your bed and walk!"

As though in a trance, the man slowly swung his legs to one side of the bed and raised himself to his feet. Standing there, the sea breeze ruffling his filthy garment, the beggar's eyes filled with tears. Silence settled over the crowd as he thrust first one foot and then the other forward, moving in a shuffling gait toward Jesus. With each step, the legs of the beggar seemed to gain new strength, and soon he was walking about on the beach, praising God and thrusting his arms outward toward the Son of Man. Shouting uncontrollably, the beggar exclaimed over and over, "Bless you, Son of David! Blessed be the name of the Lord!" Murmurs rippled throughout the crowd as the man picked up his bedroll and went away, leaping and praising God.

Before another could move toward Jesus, Jairus stepped directly before the Teacher and fell down before him, hands clasped desperately and raised toward the face of the young prophet from Nazareth.

"Master, have mercy!" he cried.

Jesus looked into the uplifted face of the ruler of the synagogue and asked simply, "What would you that I should do for you?"

"My little daughter, Master! She is even now at the point of death. Come and lay your hands upon her that she may live! I know that if you will, she can be spared, O Lord!" Jairus wept openly.

Touching the quaking shoulder of Jairus, Jesus said, "I will come to her. Show me where she is. Fear not; only believe."

Jairus felt a surge of new hope. He rose and led the way through the multitude, toward the house that adjoined the synagogue on the hill. As Jesus followed Jairus, the throng fell in behind them, talking and gesturing among themselves concerning this prophet who had risen among them.

While they were ascending the gently sloping hillside, men and women continued to join the numbers who followed doggedly behind the young healer. The press of the crowd was so great that the disciples had to move at a lively gait to avoid being trampled. A festive mood prevailed as the spectators hurried to watch the next display of divine power.

There was no gaiety in the heart of Jairus as he thought of his little twelve-year-old so near death. His lips moved slightly in prayer. Jairus felt a hand upon his shoulder and looked up at the ruggedly handsome features of the Son of Man, who said softly, "Courage, Jairus. All will be well."

As the procession topped the brow of the hill, a small woman, who had been working her way laboriously toward the forefront of the throng, now emerged into the slight clearing that separated Jesus from the huge crowd. Seizing her opportunity, she raced forward past the others, into a position directly behind the Lord. In her heart, she reflected on the twelve years during which she had suffered with a condition characterized by severe bleeding. It did not matter now that she had spent her life's savings on the futile services of physicians. If she could only reach out and touch the garments of the Lord Jesus, she knew she would receive healing. She trotted along behind him for some time, unable to bring herself to make the move toward his vesture.

Then, forsaking all caution, she lunged forward and the tips of her fingers brushed slightly across the loose cloak that Jesus always wore. In that instant, she was impressed with the exhilarating feeling that she was perfectly whole. Her spirit leaped for joy as she realized that her faith in this man from Galilee had actually resulted in her healing.

Her joy was short-lived, however, for the Teacher stopped and swung about to face the multitude. Cringing in fear, she allowed herself to be swallowed up in the throng.

"Someone touched my clothes. Who was it?" Jesus demanded.

The disciples looked at each other. There were so many people pressing around them that it was impossible to detect the person or persons who might have touched the cloak of Jesus. Their only word was, "Master, there are so many. How could you tell if someone touched you?" But Jesus continued to search the crowd. The disciples finally persuaded him to continue the journey to the home of Jairus, and the throng surged forward. Still, the Lord seemed bothered and kept turning and looking back.

Finally, unable to contain her secret longer and fearful that she might be detected under less favorable conditions the woman burst from the crowd and raced toward Jesus. Flinging herself to the ground before him, she blurted out, "It was I, Master, who touched your cloak. I have been ill for many years, but today I am well because I touched your garment." Trembling, she lifted her eyes and said to Jesus, "Bless you, Jesus, Son of David!"

Jesus touched her head lightly and said, "My daughter, your faith has made you whole. Go in peace."

Before this dramatic scene had ended, several people came out of the house of Jairus, where the night-long vigil had been held for the sick child.

One of the men of Jairus' congregation approached him and said sympathetically, "Jairus, your daughter has just died. You need not detain the Teacher longer."

At this, Jairus seemed to crumple from within. He buried his face in his hands and wept, his sobbing shaking his exhausted body.

Jesus' arm enveloped the shoulders of Jairus and he spoke quietly, "Do not be afraid, my friend. Only believe."

Quickly Jesus summoned Peter, James, and John to accompany him into the house. Jairus stood alone, head down and weeping, as some from the crowd sought to comfort him.

Wails greeted the men as they entered the house. Jesus spoke above the din and asked, "What is the meaning of this confusion?"

This rather rude approach startled the Jews who were mourning the death of one so young. Someone asked, "Who are you? What affair is this of yours? Go away if you have no sympathy for this good man and his family."

Ignoring their inhospitable manner, Jesus continued, "Why are you weeping? the girl is not dead; she is asleep!"

Guffaws and sneers greeted this remark. One man offered, "I was in the room when the physician pronounced her dead!"

"Who do you think you are, a physician? Or maybe you are God himself!" snapped another. Laughter rippled through the house as Jesus stood, calmly waiting for the confusion to die away.

Stepping to the door, he called Jairus to come inside.

Two men helped the synagogue official toward the door, where Jesus stood waiting. Turning to the mourners within, Jesus ordered, "Leave us! Go weep outside, for death has no place here!"

Amid mumblings and disgruntled remarks, the people from the house joined the multitude outside and waited.

Taking Jairus and his wife, Peter, James, and John with him, Jesus led the way to the room where the girl lay in the quietness of death. When they saw her, the parents broke out with renewed weeping, the mother crumpling to the floor. As Jairus leaned down to assist his wife, he heard the familiar authoritative voice sounding clear and strong: "Little girl, I say unto you, arise!"

Absolute silence followed. Jairus and his wife stared as though in a stupor, for there before them was an incredible sight! At the words of the Master, the child began to move slightly. Her eyes opened slowly, and her flesh took on the color of radiant health. Looking around as though waking from a pleasant dream, the girl smiled at her parents, offering her hands to them. Jairus and his overjoyed wife rushed to their daughter's side and, taking her hands, lifted her gently to the floor. The girl began walking around, not only restored to life but completely healed.

Jesus asked that food be brought for the girl and prepared to leave. Jairus rushed to the Master. "What can I say? What can I say?" he implored.

"Give God the glory, Jairus. Remember, only believe."

"How can I ever forget?" said the grateful ruler of the synagogue.

Many of the multitude who had waited outside filed into the house as Jesus and his disciples were leaving. They were speechless as they beheld a very hungry little girl stuffing her mouth with food.

Sight at Siloam

Based on John 9:1-7

The two men hastily dressed Hazor and prepared to carry him between them to the roadside near the sheep pool. This daily task had been the responsibility of Eli and Joab for as long as they could remember, for their brother had been born blind and was forced, of necessity, to ask alms of passersby in the marketplace. This he had done for the larger part of his twenty years.

As the boys grew older, this chore had become an odious one, though they loved their younger brother and often wished that there was more they could do for him. They chafed beneath the stigma of poverty, as did most of the residents of this section of Jerusalem. The family barely subsisted on the meager wages of the father, Asa, whose trade was that of a tanner. Their own paltry earnings as camel drivers failed to yield more than a bare existence. Yet the attitude of the family toward their economic condition was far from hopeless resignation. They held fast to their Jewish traditions and looked forward to the time when their people would be free from the tyranny of Roman rule.

After seating Hazor at his accustomed station in the great marketplace, the brothers walked along the crowded, narrow street. At length they came to the area where the camel drivers selected workers to help them on the long journey to Nazareth, near the Sea of Galilee.

Eli touched Joab's arm and spoke above the confusion of the crowd. "Joab, wait. I wish to speak with you a moment."

Joab's dark eyes and swarthy complexion were enhanced by the growth of a magnificent beard that lent an air of dignity to his countenance. Eli stood a full head taller than his younger brother and was more powerfully built. He too wore a beard, but it was short, with a tinge of gray showing here and there.

This day Eli was particularly concerned over the plight of Hazor, and as he spoke, his words were heavy with emotion.

"Joab, I know that you must feel as I about Hazor and his affliction. We both love our brother and wish him to be as other men. And," he continued earnestly, "I learned only yesterday of someone who perhaps can help him. I feel that if our brother could meet this man, he might even have his sight restored."

A long moment passed as Joab studied the face of his brother. The crowd, which continually jostled past the merchants' stalls, pressed rudely against the two, in their determination to be among the first to purchase the fresh meats and vegetables in the marketplace.

"Eli, this is no place to talk. I can barely hear you. Let us walk over to that old building where it will be quieter."

The two made their way toward an ancient building, now in an advanced state of decay. They sat down on a broken slab of stone which lay at the entrance. The morning sunlight engulfed them as they sat looking at the constant stream of people going past.

"You were saying something about a man who could help Hazor," began Joab quizzically. "Eli, you know full well our family has no money for physicians. No one can do anything for him except to drop an extra coin in his hand."

Eli leaned forward and said in a low voice, "Joab, there is a man, lately come from Galilee, who is reported to be able to make the lame walk and the blind see. I've seen him from a distance—yesterday, when I went to look for work on the fishing boats at the Sea of Tiberias."

Joab's eyes narrowed to slits as he listened with the ear of a skeptic. He motioned for Eli to continue.

Eli spoke excitedly now as he described his experience of the previous day. "He was speaking to a large gathering of people on the shore. I did not hear much of what he was saying because the boat put out to sea, but I feel that he is able to help Hazor. I *know* he is, Joab."

Joab stopped him with a coarse laugh. "Eli, surely you don't mean the vagabond carpenter from Nazareth, the man called Jesus! Why, he has been put out of the synagogue for teaching against the traditions of our fathers. He is headed for real trouble, that fellow. Our priest said only last Sabbath that we are not to put any stock in the teachings of that magician. Just don't tell Hazor and get his hopes up, whatever you do!" exclaimed Joab, fastening a latchet of his sandal.

Eli felt rather foolish for having mentioned the controversial preacher, but he felt immeasurably worse for having been censored by his younger brother. Yet he felt in his heart that this one who called himself the Son of Man possessed some strange power to do good for all men.

Joab rose quickly and said as they rejoined the bustling multitudes in the marketplace, "I wish to help Hazor as much as you, but I am not so foolish as to listen to rumor and believe the impossible! Come, we had better find Jehu the camel driver and see if he has work for us today."

As the brother gained the opposite side of the square, a group of excited children burst from among the crowd, several stray dogs yapping beside them as they ran toward the place where Eli and Joab stood. Their shouts of "The Teacher comes! The Teacher comes!" brought the two men to a halt. They looked toward the eastern edge of the city, alongside of which ran the roadway where they had left Hazor earlier that morning.

Now their attention centered on the noisy children who were proclaiming the approach into the city of the famed carpenter from Nazareth.

"Joab, they mean Jesus!" exclaimed Eli to his brother, who was wearing a frown of disapproval. "Don't you understand? He is the man I was telling you about who is reported to be able to heal! Let us go and watch for him," persisted Eli.

Joab had decided long ago that he would remain faithful to the Mosaic law as prescribed by the temple priest and was quite obstinate in his refusal to accompany Eli to the roadside. He turned and walked away quickly with the admonition, "There are some things more important than listening to the idle talk of a wandering preacher!"

Eli allowed himself to be shoved along in the general direction of the public square where hundreds now lined the roadway on both sides hoping for a glimpse of the young miracle worker.

The teeming multitude reminded Eli of the crowds that were wont to frequent the sports arenas within the city, erected by their Roman conquerors to stage chariot races and athletic events.

Abruptly, his thoughts were interrupted as a number of people appeared in the distance, walking along the well-traveled road which led into Jerusalem. In the vanguard walked a young bearded man, robed in a white tunic. Several men, who seemed to be approximately the same age as the man in the lead, clustered about him and spoke with him familiarly from time to time.

As they neared the place where Eli stood in the midst of the crowd, these men lined out along both sides of the road, admonishing the crowds to make way. Occasionally they would shout at someone who happened to wander into the path of the advancing group.

The hot Jerusalem sun now beamed down unmercifully, and as Eli pushed his way to the outer edge of the throng he could see beads of perspiration on the forehead of the famous young prophet. There was a fixed look upon the uplifted countenance of this young man whom some regarded as the Son of God. He seemed preoccupied, as though unaware of the presence of the crowds of spectators. To Eli, it seemed that indeed this man was upon a mission of divine import; his bearing bespoke majestic dignity, not unlike that of a king.

As the Teacher strode past the cluster of people where Eli stood, he suddenly turned his head in Eli's direction. For a fleeting moment, Eli felt strangely alone—singled out by that searching glance, somehow suspended in time and space—an emotion with which he was totally unfamiliar. He was not a particularly religious man, as was Joab. Yet there was something in that glance which drew him to the man called Jesus.

The swarm of people became more intent now in their collective determination to obtain a closer view of this famous personage. They pressed forward, moving Eli with them. The mass of humanity converged into a solid wall behind Jesus and the disciples as they continued their journey which was leading them directly into the busy marketplace.

Merchants and hawkers paused in their quest for customers as they stared blankly at the tumult on the dusty road. Clearly, Jesus was the center of attraction as he came into the busiest sector of the marketplace.

Eli had now entirely forgotten his plan to seek employment; he was irresistibly drawn along with the multitude toward the place where the Teacher had come to a halt. Jesus was surrounded by his disciples, who had succeeded in creating an open space among the throng.

Eli noted that the crowd had gathered near the place where he and Joab had left Hazor earlier to pursue his miserable occupation. With determination, Eli pushed his way to the edge of the crush of spectators. He had managed to reach a spot a short distance from Jesus when he saw that the Master was standing directly in front of the blind Hazor.

There was a look of unmistakable compassion upon the face of Jesus as he beheld the plight of the beggar who was totally unaware of his presence. Hazor continued his plea for alms, his sightless eyes importuning any who might cast a coin into the basket he grasped in a thin hand.

Suddenly, a disciple leaned toward the Teacher and spoke softly. Eli strained to hear above the commotion about him. He caught bits of the conversation and was trying to inch his way closer when one of the disciples, thinking Eli intended to distract Jesus in some manner, moved to his side and touched his arm in admonition. Eli turned and recognized James, a brother of the young prophet from Nazareth.

"Please do not interrupt the Master, for he is very busy today. He goes to Capernaum to teach, and must leave Jerusalem within the hour," was the disciple's request.

Realizing that he must present his case quickly and with conviction, he pleaded, "That man! There on the ground. He is my brother! Please, I must get closer so that I can ask the Teacher to help him. I know he can help my brother!" His eyes burned with the earnestness of his cause, but he sensed that he was making no headway with the resolute James who maintained his hold on Eli's garment.

At that moment, another disciple made his way through the crowd toward Eli and James. He was a large, bronzed man, one who apparently had labored hard at some manual occupation. His arms were brawny and his large hands were rough from exposure to the elements. He wore a short-cropped beard which lent a kind of ferociousness to his already commanding appearance.

"Peter," began James dubiously, "this man claims to be the brother of the one seated there before the Master. He wishes to speak with Jesus concerning the beggar."

The large man looked upon Eli with a practiced eye. His bearing was that of a man skilled in the art of dealing with men.

"Is it true what you say of the beggar to whom our Master has chosen to give of his time?" demanded the second disciple.

"Yes," replied Eli quickly. "His name is Hazor, and it is true that I am his brother." He continued gamely, "If I could but speak to the Teacher, I am certain that he could help him!"

Peter looked toward Jesus and started to say something to him. But already the piercing eyes of the Son of Man were searching out those of Eli, who stood transfixed at the inner edge of the throng.

"Come," commanded Jesus as he stretched forth his hand toward Eli, whose heart now raced wildly. It was with some difficulty that Eli suppressed a desire to turn back into the protective mass of people and hide from that disturbingly steady gaze.

Slowly the grip which James held upon Eli's arm loosened, and Peter motioned for Eli to go forward.

"Please!" blurted Eli. "My brother was born without sight. Cause him to see, O Lord!"

Speaking with an authority that almost frightened Eli, Jesus replied, "I perceive that you have faith, and faith is given unto you of my Father."

Sensing the note of hope in the Master's voice, Eli

persisted in presenting his brother's case. "I believe with all my heart that you are the very Son of God. I am convinced that you have power over all things," Eli heard himself confess.

Turning to Hazor, Jesus spoke to Eli, "Because you believe, you shall behold the power of God."

The pleas for alms had stopped now as Hazor seemed to realize that he was in the presence of some awesome power. A look of bewilderment and expectancy etched itself upon his features.

A disciple who had been regarding the blind beggar now spoke. "Lord, who sinned, this man or his parents, that he was born blind?" It was commonly supposed among the Jews that illness or misfortune was duly visited upon those who had violated one or more of the commandments as given by Moses. Indeed, it must extend, according to traditional belief, to the second and third generations.

Jesus softly replied, "Neither this man nor his parents have sinned to cause this blindness. Rather, it was done that the glory of the Father might be shown through him. I must perform the works of him who sent me while it is yet day; the night comes on, when no man can work. As long as I am in the world, I am the light of the world."

As Jesus finished speaking, dissension spread among the crowd. Some argued vociferously that Jesus was a madman and blasphemed. Others, clamoring just as loudly, declared that he was a prophet who healed by the power of God.

Jesus perceived the commotion and raised his hand in a gesture for silence. The tumult ceased and attention once more focused upon the two principals, Jesus the controversial Teacher and Hazor the blind beggar.

Suddenly, Jesus lowered himself to one knee before the puzzled blind man. He then ceremoniously spat upon the ground before him, stirring a mixture from the red dust of the roadway. Dipping a finger into the swirl of moist clay, he brought it close to the face of Hazor. Tenderly, he touched one eye and then the other, wiping the clay-like substance in a horizontal movement across the closed, blind orbs.

He spoke gently but with unquestionable authority to Hazor as he laid his hand lightly upon the frail shoulder of the blind beggar. "Go, friend, and wash your eyes in the pool of Siloam."

The outlet of the pool flowed into the Kidron Valley, which separated the city of Jerusalem from the Mount of Olives on the east. It had been variously used as a sheep pool and as a public water supply and was only a few yards away.

Simeon, a disciple, stood beside Hazor and helped the blind man to his feet. Hazor rose slowly and stood uncertainly, fingering in wonder the cool mass of clay upon his sightless eyes. He then groped his way through the crowd, muttering in a low voice.

Several disciples were now attempting to clear a path for him through the mass of spectators, while Simeon helped Hazor toward the water.

Meanwhile, Jesus stood watching the two men as they pressed their way to the pool.

The surface of the water reflected the faces of Simeon and Hazor as they bowed themselves toward its coolness. Simeon left Hazor on his knees at the pool's edge and looked back toward Jesus, who motioned for him to return.

Hesitantly, Hazor cupped his hands and lowered them slowly into the stream. He felt the cold water work its way past his wrists, and he held his hands beneath the surface for a long moment. Summoning his courage, the blind man withdrew his hands and quickly dashed the silvery spray into his eyes. The clay trickled down his cheeks in a thin watery line of reddish brown. Again and again Hazor dipped into the water, slowly bathing both eyes with the cool liquid.

As he blinked the last drops from the edges of his eyes, he suddenly beheld himself staring into the face of a stranger in the water. He stretched his hands toward the reflection and touched the surface. Instantly the ripples reflected the brilliant sunlight in a million sparkling pinpoints. He grinned at himself in the water, and stood, reveling in the sheer ecstasy of sight. He turned toward the crowd and looked in delighted amazement at his new world. Walking as though in a dream, he strode toward the center of the multitude, where Jesus stood with outstretched arm.

Falling to his knees, Hazor took the hands of the Master and buried his face in them, weeping openly with joy and gratitude. Still clutching the hands of his benefactor, he slowly raised his eyes and looked upon Jesus.

Hazor was unprepared for the question posed by this strange man who had restored his sight. Jesus asked pointedly, "Hazor, do you believe on the Son of God?"

With confusion marking his reply, he who had been blind replied, "Who is he, Lord, that I might believe?"

Jesus answered in measured tone, "You have both seen him and talked with him. He it is that now speaks with you."

Hazor's eyes riveted upon the face of Jesus, carpenter from Nazareth. At last, he managed to utter, "Lord, I believe!" Stinging tears of thanksgiving now bathed the eyes which once were blind, as Hazor knelt in the dust of the roadway near the pool called Siloam.

Lazarus: Profile of Resurrection

Based on John 11:1-46

Mary recalled vividly the difficulty with which she and her sister Martha had saved the money out of their meager earnings to purchase the fragrant spikenard. The fact that the aromatic ointment had been quite expensive and that there had been much criticism of her extravagance in pouring it freely over the travel-weary feet of her Lord had not deterred her in her purpose. Hers had been an act of pure worship, born of a knowledge that eternal values far outweigh any monetary consideration; and she loved her Lord above all else on earth. Hence her tears and humility of spirit as she had proceeded to dry with her long hair the feet of the One who bore the imprint of eternity in his very being.

This ancient Eastern custom of recognition and welcome took on a holy and eternal significance that day. The Christ memorialized her efforts, saying to those gathered about, "This woman, by her act of worship, has shown proof that her sins have truly been forgiven." In this manner the Lord taught the value of thankful worship in connection with the forgiveness of sin.

It was no secret to any of her acquaintances that hers had been a life of degradation and shame before she had met the Master. The caustic criticism of some who beheld this simple rite failed to diminish her love for this man who had understood her far better than any on earth had ever done.

So it was that a bond of comradeship had been formed between Jesus and his friends at Bethany—Mary, Martha, and their brother Lazarus.

Jesus and Lazarus had often walked the sunlit hills and valleys of Bethany discussing things pertaining to the kingdom of God. On one such occasion Lazarus had witnessed the hostility of the religious leaders of Jewry toward the simple message of love that his friend had preached to them. The temple priest from Bethany had been arguing a point of law in the Mosaic code. His face had turned livid with rage as he condemned Jesus and threatened to oust from the congregation of the synagogue those who dared believe his doctrine. Some who had been swayed by the anger of the priest had turned back toward the village, leaving Jesus and Lazarus to their tormentors. Stones had been hastily gathered by these zealots of the law and threats had increased among those who claimed to be the preservers of the integrity of the law.

Jesus had calmly pierced their shell of hypocrisy. At that moment the power of God had confronted those advocates of traditional religion and their interpretation of the Law of Moses. In an instantaneous flash of heavenly power the enemies of the Son of Man had become immobilized, totally unable to hurl their stones of hatred and prejudice. With a soft "Mine hour is not yet come," Jesus and Lazarus had moved unscathed from their midst.

As they walked together along the dusty road to the next village, Lazarus had grieved for his friend and felt shame for the behavior of his fellows. The look of sorrow he had beheld on the countenance of the Master had brought tears to his eyes. Their friendship had ripened into an abiding love and concern, and the prayers of Lazarus for the safety of his friend had not ceased from that day forward.

Now Jesus sat reading a parchment, scribbled in haste, which had just arrived from Bethany. Thomas ceased mending his nets and strode to the far side of the small room where Jesus sat staring at the parchment. Several other disciples, concern working into their hearts, gathered about the Teacher. The glow from a single candle deepened the furrows of anxiety on their faces.

Presently Jesus looked up and said evenly, "Lazarus is sick in Bethany. But the end result of this illness will be unto the glory of God."

"Master, Bethany is the town where the Jews only recently threatened your life. Surely you do not plan to expose yourself to such danger again!" exclaimed Matthew.

Jesus laid the message on the table before them and said no more.

After the second day had passed and Jesus had made no effort to undertake the journey to Bethany, the disciples began to relax and slowly returned to their normal routine.

At the end of the fourth day, however, Jesus gathered about himself the little band of believers, drawn as they were from various pursuits in the Jewish community, and laid his plan before them.

Thomas once again implored Jesus to reconsider when it was learned that he planned to return after all to the village of Bethany to visit the family of Lazarus.

Jesus, motivated as always by a higher power than the counsel of men, spoke in tones of authority. "A day has twelve hours, doesn't it, Thomas?" he began. "As long as a man walks in daylight he has no occasion of stumbling because he sees the light of this world, the sun in the heavens. But if he walks in the night, he may very well stumble and fall, for the light has ceased to shine." Jesus perceived their finite grasp of what he was saying, but continued, "Our friend Lazarus has fallen on sleep. I will go and awaken him."

Quickly the disciples, to whom sleep had become a luxury due to their constant ministry and narrow escapes from the Jews, responded, "Lord, if he is asleep, he will rest and recover."

The Lord knew that their thoughts centered on the physical benefits of natural sleep, so he stated bluntly, "Lazarus sleeps the sleep of death; he is dead."

At this, Matthew's eyes narrowed into slits as he tried to take in the full import of this announcement. Lazarus had been one of his dearest friends, also.

"I am glad for your sakes that I was not there," Jesus went on, "in order that you might believe more readily that which is to follow."

Thomas, puzzled and with unbridled concern now coloring his words, exclaimed to the others, "If our Master is intent upon making this journey, then let us all go with him that at least we may have the honor of dying with him!"

The crude wooden door of a fishing shack in Jerusalem closed slowly behind the last of the little group as they made their way toward Bethany and possible martyrdom.

. . . . .

Small birds sang sweetly from the olive trees as Jesus and his timorous band of disciples strode toward the tiny village of Bethany, situated on the side of the Mount of Olives.

A messenger was dispatched from the home of Mary and Martha to inform Jesus that Lazarus had indeed died and that he had been buried four days earlier. Jesus accepted this news with calmness tempered with sorrow and continued his walk toward the humble home of his friends.

Martha, eyes swollen from grief, first received the news that Jesus was advancing toward the village. Hurriedly she made her way through the concourse of Jews who had come the short distance from Jerusalem to console the sisters and ran toward the outskirts of the village. Martha's burdened heart bared itself in the presence of the Son of Man as she clung to his tunic. With charged emotions she blurted out, "Lord, if you had been here, my brother would not have died!" Quickly she regained her faith in the matchless Teacher and continued, "But I know that even now God will grant you whatever you ask of him."

Her clutch upon his vesture became more intense. Gently Jesus put Martha from him and looked into her brimming eyes.

"Your brother shall rise again," he whispered softly.

"I know, Lord," she replied sobbing. "I know he will rise again to life on the last day. I know, but it is so hard to go on living without him!"

With infinite patience, Jesus said evenly, "I am the resurrection and the life. Whoever believes in me shall live, even though he dies, and whoever lives and believes on me shall never die. Do you believe this, Martha?"

At this she straightened, and with a resurgence of strength, said simply, "Yes, Lord! I believe that you are the Messiah, the Son of God!"

Jesus encircled her shoulders with hands of infinite strength and gentleness.

While Jesus and his disciples were yet some distance from the village, Martha left her place beside the Lord and ran toward the house where Mary sat still grieving.

"The Master is here," she announced excitedly, "and he is asking for you, Mary!"

Mary followed her sister outside, alternately running and walking toward the place where Jesus had halted just short of the village.

Many of the Jews, thinking that she was returning to the sepulcher to weep, followed Mary. When they saw Jesus, however, they stopped. They exchanged glances of disapproval as the sisters ran toward the Lord.

Falling in a heap at the feet of the Master, Mary wept bitterly. So great was the bereavement of the moment that many of the Jews wept with her as Mary voiced the plaintive cry of her sister, "If you had been here, Lord, my brother would not have died!"

Caught in the sorrow of that moment, the humanity of the Lord Jesus broke forth, and he wept.

Even the hypercritical Jews perceived the deep love Jesus had for his friend Lazarus, for they remarked among themselves, "Behold, how he loved him!" Others, critical of spiritual values, spat out, "He opened the eyes of the blind. Could he not have prevented the death of his friend?"

Without further comment Jesus looked up and asked, "Where have you buried him?"

The sisters took him by the hand and led him to the sepulcher. It was hewn from solid stone, with a short flight of steps descending into the burial vault. Jesus stood alone before the entrance and commanded the stone to be removed.

Martha interrupted these preparations with a warning. "Lord, he has been dead for four days now. There will be a terrible odor if you have the stone removed!"

Jesus reprimanded her quietly: "Did I not say to you that you would see the glory of God, if only you believe?"

Sunlight filtered into the blackness of the burial chamber as several of the men moved the huge, unwieldy stone.

Completely exposed now, the gloom of the place of death confronted Jesus as he lifted his face toward heaven.

"Father," he began confidently, "I thank you that you do always hear me. I know that you do always hear me, but I said this because of these who stand here, that they might believe that you have indeed sent me."

Thomas, standing with the other disciples, half-expected a terrifying earthquake or some other dramatic phenomenon to attend these words of his Master.

Probably none of them there that day—Jews, sisters, or disciples—really expected that which next took place. With a majestic upward sweep of his hand, Jesus exclaimed with a loud voice, "Lazarus! Come forth!"

No sound save that of a twittering sparrow broke the silence. Hushed expectancy settled upon them all.

Suddenly, sunlight washed over the emerging figure of a man, wrapped mummy-like from head to foot, walking slowly up the steps.

Quickly and lovingly Lazarus was freed from his graveclothes and restored to his family and friends. As the crowd moved away, Lazarus walking majestically in their midst, a small breeze ruffled a pile of white linen lying before an empty tomb.

The Ear of Malchus

Based on John 18:1-11

Malchus sat in deep contemplation in the deserted courtyard where he served as bond slave to the high priest Caiaphas. The vast cobblestone area about him lay adjacent to the Via Dolorosa, the infamous "Way of Sorrow" in the ancient city of Jerusalem. This was the dirty, narrow street through which a troublemaker by the name of Jesus from the town of Nazareth had been jostled and shoved toward the dreaded place of execution known as Golgotha, the "Place of the Skull."

It had not been the first of such criminal executions and very probably would not be the last. Trouble seethed within the city and a pall of doom had seemed to hang over the town since the death of Jesus, also called Christ.

Malchus recalled the fury of the mob that night. Most of those involved had seemingly lost all control. The fate of the young preacher whom some regarded as a prophet and whom some looked upon as the Son of God had hung in the balance. Tempers had flared, friends had become bitter enemies, and old enemies like Pilate and Herod had become friends. Throughout the mockery of a trial, it was clearly evident that the mob had wanted blood. They had shouted down every objection put forth by Pilate in defense of the man Jesus in whom he could find no wrong.

Malchus recalled, too, how he himself had been swept along with the current and was tempted to join in the shout of "Away with him! Crucify him! Crucify him!"

Time and again Pilate, the Roman procurator, had attempted to dissuade the unruly mob as they rained insults and false charges upon the accused carpenter from Nazareth. This was immediately met with violence and new outbursts of rage as well as political threats against Pilate and his secure position as governor of Judea. These intimidations had finally broken the will of Pilate and he had acquiesced to their demand that Jesus be bound over to them for crucifixion—the supreme penalty under Roman law.

In his mind's eye Malchus could still see the water from the copper basin in which Pontius Pilate had symbolically washed his hands, trickling among the cobblestones of the courtyard. Pilate had hurled the water after the mob as it quickly melted away toward Golgotha, sweeping along with it the one called Christ.

Malchus remembered the rage on the tortured features of Pilate as he had turned and looked upon the solitary figure standing in the courtyard below the seat of judgment. Barabbas, formerly condemned to suffer crucifixion for having led an insurrection against Roman tyranny, gazed in wonder at the constant stream of humanity making its way to the edge of the city. He was free; another was now laboring beneath the heavy means of his own torture and death.

Barabbas rubbed his swollen wrists, so recently freed from their heavy shackles, and walked slowly out of the place of judgment.

Malchus reflected on the events that had preceded the mock trial. He struggled to justify what had happened and his own participation in the sorry spectacle.

His mind flashed back to that night, less than a week

before, when his master the high priest had summoned him to the sanctuary. There he was instructed to accompany several men of the city on a mission to collect what weapons might be found hidden and to issue them to a delegation preparing to assist in the arrest of a religious fanatic.

The Roman governor had forbidden weapons of any description to be kept in the homes of the common people of the city of Jerusalem through fear of an armed uprising. This was not an unlikely possibility, as witness the recent revolution led by a firebrand named Barabbas, now condemned to face execution.

Malchus had done as he was told. Swords and lanterns and long wooden staves were procured from several homes and at last the men were ready to begin their search.

Someone from the crowd shouted, "Judas said for us to meet him and the soldiers at the Brook Kidron. There he'll tell us where to find Jesus of Nazareth!"

Malchus wanted no part of this pack of madmen. He turned to go back to his quarters when a large man, wearing a Roman battle helmet though obviously not a soldier, grabbed his arm and snarled, "We need all the help we can get tonight! Come with me!" A stave was thrust into his hands, and thus was Malchus swept along toward the rendezvous with Judas Iscariot and the soldiers.

The very air was charged with excitement as the group waited for Judas at the appointed place, a small brook which ran through the city on the east. Impatiently they glanced down the road for any sign of Iscariot and the reinforcements he was supposed to be bringing. Meanwhile, others from the city joined the increasing number of men.

"I don't trust that fellow Judas!" one man said as he lighted his torch. "He's a double-dealer, that's what he is! Why, he's one of them himself! How do we know he is telling us the truth?"

Another echoed this note of distrust: "If he doesn't show up here tonight, he had better make plans to leave this city forever!"

Shouts and grunts of assent rose from the crowd.

Suddenly, a glow of light could be seen around a bend in the road leading up to the crossing. The clank of swords against the steel body plates of Roman soldiers pierced the darkness as the second group approached. In the forefront of the column of soldiers walked a young man, his face triumphant beneath the unsteady glow of the torches held by the guides.

The two groups quickly merged into a single company under the command of a Roman centurion.

Judas spoke to the commander, "He will be found in the garden, beyond the brook." Malchus noted an air of superiority in the tone of the man Iscariot as he continued to answer questions and point from time to time in the general direction of the garden area. It was quite obvious that the soldiers disliked Judas, but he apparently cared little what they thought.

"Yes! I'm sure!" continued Judas. "We often came here to the garden while our leader went into the wooded area to pray. I know for certain that he will be there tonight. He will need more than prayers when he sees the surprise we have for him, won't he, commander?"

The centurion ignored the arrogance of the remark and busied himself with giving orders in the cold, professional manner of the Roman soldier.

Suddenly they were in motion again and Malchus found himself in the forefront of the crowd, forced there by the shoving, disorderly mob as they pushed their way across the bridge.

The garden was outlined by stately trees, interlaced with

willows and flanked on the right by a group of ancient evergreens, looming black now against the evening sky.

As the crowd pressed forward in the darkness a small clearing became visible directly in their line of march. The centurion halted the advance, possibly to get his bearings before proceeding farther. Anxiously they awaited the order to move into the clearing.

The order never came. Out of the gloom stepped a stately form, robed completely in white. The man's voice rang sharp and clear in the coolness of the garden.

Malchus looked in stupefied wonder at the calm figure standing before them and his very frame seemed to melt into nothingness beneath him. The sudden appearance of Jesus had likewise affected the others, for Malchus heard hushed whispers of wonder and fear. "Is that the man we have been sent to bring in? My God! What manner of man is he?" Conversation rippled throughout the crowd. Mutterings of "Lord!" could be heard among the ranks of hardened Roman troops as a number of them lowered themselves to one knee.

Summoning his poise, the centurion stepped forward, armed with the scroll upon which was written the official order for arrest. Before he could speak, the words of the Christ flashed through the darkness, "Whom seek ye?"

"Jesus of Nazareth is the name written on this order," the centurion answered, almost apologetically.

Without hesitation, Jesus replied, "I am he."

Malchus could have sworn that some strange power proceeded from the person of this man in the garden. At any rate, some supernal force seemed to press them all to the ground. Some knelt, others covered their faces with their vestures.

Again Jesus asked the question, "Whom seek ye?"

Again the centurion found his voice and managed the

reply, "Jesus of Nazareth," as the men slowly rose to their feet.

"I have told you that I am he. If I be the one you seek, then let no harm come to these my followers." The words were spoken in what seemed to Malchus to be sheer tones of thunder.

The small band of disciples had now drawn protectively about Jesus, hesitating between flight and action. The one known as Simon Peter had secreted a sword beneath the folds of his garments. Now he swiftly brought it out, sensing the danger his Lord was in. With a swing of the vicious blade, he brought it down on the first man within reach.

Malchus had been staring down at the soft grass of the garden, ashamed to look upon this wondrous man who was possessed of such great power. He glanced up in time to see moonlight flash on the broadside of a battle sword. With a sickening slash the sharpness of the blade met the softness of human flesh and Malchus felt the hot blood stream down his neck, across his shoulder, and into his vesture. Searing, scalding pain shot through his head and he suddenly realized that it was his own bloody ear that lay at the feet of Jesus.

Malchus was in shock as he stood frozen to the spot, his hand covering the gory wound in his head. Sickness washed over him and he felt himself sinking to the ground.

The metallic scrape of steel on steel was instantly heard through the ranks as swords were drawn. Stepping forward to Peter, Jesus spoke softly. "Put up your sword, Peter. All who take the sword shall perish by the sword. Do you not know that if I asked him, the Father would even now send twelve legions of angels to do battle for me? But such is not the kingdom of God."

Malchus had now fallen to one knee and was in terrible

pain. Slowly he opened his eyes as tender, loving hands lifted him up. In utter amazement Malchus beheld Jesus stoop, pick up the severed ear, and place it tenderly against his head.

In a moment it was as though nothing had happened. The ear remained steadfast. Malchus reached up and touched it, unable to believe the healing he had just experienced. He looked at Peter who stood motionless in the paleness of the moonlight, sword held limply at his side, and saw tears trickling down the big man's cheeks.

. . . . .

Now, three days later, Malchus listened to the awful stillness of the narrow street known as the "Way of Sorrow." A hush had fallen over the entire city following the crucifixion; an aura of guilt and shame attended the daily lives of all who dwelt there.

The earthquake which had followed the death of the Christ had split the paving which surrounded the living quarters of the high priest. A zigzag crack now ran the length of the outer courtyard. Weird things were taking place in the ancient city. The high priest Caiaphas was at the temple, almost hysterical over the huge curtain that had been ripped from top to bottom at the moment of the death of Jesus. No longer was the Holy of Holies kept separate from the outer court where the common people stood while the priests entered to make sacrifice for the sins of all.

There were rumors that the man from Nazareth had risen from the dead. Some claimed the soldiers had been paid to declare that Jesus' disciples had stolen his body and hidden it. Not only that but there were stories circulating that the earthquake had broken up parts of the cemetery and that some of the dead had left their graves.

A chill wind blew against Malchus. He drew his robe more closely about him and strode across the deserted courtyard. As he looked up at the fading light in the western sky, he raised his hand and gently caressed his right ear.

Interrupted Funeral

Based on Luke 7:11-17

The bereaved mother sat at a small table, sight blurred by the tears that flooded her brown eyes. She was attended by a physician who encouraged her from time to time to drink from a small flask which he held. She had at first refused the potion, preferring to absorb the full brunt of anguish that filled her heart. Now she sipped at the green liquid and rested her head upon her arms folded upon the crude table.

As if being a widow was not hard enough she must now suffer the loss of her only son as well. The form of a young man lay upon a sleeping mat in one corner of the small hovel she had tried so hard to make a home. Several women were hovering about the corpse, weeping as they prepared it for burial.

" 'The Lord giveth, and the Lord taketh away; blessed be the name of the Lord,' " quoted the elderly physician, putting his bottles and instruments away in the leather pack he carried. He placed his hand upon the shoulder of the sorrowing mother and wagged his head in helpless resignation. Walking to the door, he opened it quietly and prepared to leave. There in the early morning light was the bulky figure of a Roman soldier about to rap on the door. His two companions waited respectfully at the edge of the narrow street. The physician brushed past the soldier who entered unbidden.

"By the decree of Herod, I am commanded to secure the name of the deceased for the public record," he announced as he removed a scroll of parchment and a quill from a round metal case slung about his shoulder.

The widow looked up at the official and asked in a broken voice, "How did you know he was dead? Is nothing sacred to you but your records?"

"News of death takes wings, dear lady. The physicians of this village have instructions to report cases of patients who are dying—even an Israelite! This physician so informed me before coming to this house," he said in a detached and professional manner.

"His name was Jehu," the woman replied. "He lived a mere fifteen years, and now he is gone forever!"

The soldier recorded the name with deft strokes of the quill, rolled the parchment and placed it in its holder. Turning to leave, he spoke more kindly, "My sympathy, woman, but perhaps it is better to lose him thusly than to have him die in battle." With that, he closed the rough-hewn door and rejoined the others.

Several women now clustered about the sobbing mother, seeking to render consolation.

"Now I have no one!" she cried as she buried her face in the folds of a friend's garment.

Tall candles, their steady flame appearing to be pasted against the darkness of the room, stood in place around the body of Jehu, young Israelite, dead at fifteen.

. . . . .

Having passed the night in prayer, Jesus and several disciples were returning from Capernaum to the city of Nain, to the south. Their journey had brought them in contact with many who sought the healing ministry of the Son of Man. Many there were also whose sole desire it was to behold the miraculous and to feed upon the physical provisions the Lord sometimes made available to them.

Of course there were those who, upon hearing the matchless words of Jesus as he spoke to them on the mountainside, became stalwart and earnest believers and determined to follow him. These had accompanied him as far as Nain, forsaking family and friends in their quest for that bread of life which seemed to inhere in this wondrous stranger from Nazareth.

One of this group was a former tax collector by the name of Matthew, sometimes called Levi. His encounter with Jesus had been traumatic and brief. Seated at his appointed place for the purpose of garnering taxes for Imperial Rome, he had looked up one day expecting to see yet another Israelite whose coins would be added to the growing pile.

Matthew was never the same after that look into the face of divinity. In his consternation he had heard the simple, clear command, "Follow me." Without a backward glance, Matthew had walked out on his past, completely enthralled by the magnetism of the Teacher.

It was Matthew who saw the mourners, coffin preceding their weary, doleful way to the outskirts of the village. It was he, too, who was most surprised at the reaction of the Master as he encountered this procession of death. Tradition would compel one to step aside respectfully, but when Jesus moved into the path of the funeral party and halted it, Matthew could only gaze in open-mouthed astonishment.

The silence that followed was broken only by the creaking of the wooden poles of the bier and the soft weeping of the mother of young Jehu. Stepping to her side, Jesus smiled confidently and said, "Woman, weep not."

Mutterings of disapproval at this intrusion rippled

through the funeral party. One man challenged Jesus: "Make way, carpenter! Save your words of comfort for the service at the grave!"

Brushing past him, Jesus walked to the bier, still borne upon the shoulders of four young men. Stretching forth his hand, the Teacher touched the rough wood of the casket.

"Young man!" rang the voice of Jesus in the cool morning air, "I say unto you, Arise!"

Somewhere in the distance, the mournful clang of a funeral bell reverberated upon the stillness. No one dared move.

Then, almost imperceptibly, the heavy lid of the casket began a slow upward motion, resting finally in an upright position. A gasp spread throughout the ranks of those who had beheld this incredible thing happen.

Hands appeared on the rims of the coffin, knuckles whitening under the pressure of the rising figure within the narrow box. Sitting upright above the startled crowd, Jehu looked about him in amazement.

Joyfully, the men lowered their burden to the ground. Jesus took the boy's arm as he stepped from the coffin to the firmness of the earth.

The mother whose son had been restored threw her arms about him and wept in the ecstasy of the miraculous. Her eyes fell upon Jesus and she cried out, "God himself has truly come among his people! Praise the name of Jehovah!"

From a heaping mound of earth in the cemetery, a slim trickle of dirt plunged to the bottom of an empty grave.

Angel of Deliverance

Based on Acts 12

Eleven years had passed since James had seen the risen Lord at the Sea of Tiberias. Could he ever forget the wonder that flooded his aching heart that morning? He and the others had followed in bewilderment the instructions of the stranger on the shore, only to land the most tremendous catch of fish of their lives. He smiled to himself as he recalled the dumbfounded expression on the face of Peter when he realized that it was really Jesus standing on the shore. Peter's reaction was typical of that impulsive fisherman. He had hastily grabbed up his short leather fisher's coat, wrapped it about his naked body, and poised himself on the bow of the ship. Without so much as a second glance, he had hurled his massive body into the sea to hide himself from the Lord.

James remembered, too, the day that he was privileged to accompany the Lord and Peter and his brother John to the pinnacle of a high mountain near the city of Jerusalem. There he had become an eyewitness to glory as he beheld the Lord Jesus speaking with the Father and the prophets. He held in sacred memory the glory that had bathed the Master, whose very countenance shone with the splendor of heaven itself.

Now James the Apostle sat in a foul prison in Jerusalem. From time to time, large rats scurried across his swollen ankles, clamped fast with irons connected to the filthy wall by a chain. He had long since become accustomed to his surroundings. He saw without seeing the scrawled letters of the name of some former unfortunate, along with a profusion of lewd drawings and an occasional calendar date chipped into the sandstone wall.

Constructed to contain no more than ten prisoners, the cold stone cell was now jammed with eighteen men—or what had formerly been men. Unbelievable filth abounded in the stinking darkness that now constituted James's world.

His crime had been a chance remark to a group of citizens that one day Christ would be king over all the earth. A relative of the vicious Claudius, emperor of Imperial Rome, happened to be in the crowd. Word was hastily dispatched to the palace that James was plotting to overthrow the Roman government of Judea. His arrest had been swift and violent, as soldiers dragged him from the home of his brother, John, in the small hours of the morning.

A heavy metal door slammed somewhere above the winding stone stairway, and the unmistakable crunch of footsteps upon the paved atrium which led to the stairs echoed down to the hollow dungeon area. James, his face ashen and drawn and eyes hollow from three months in the prison of Herod Agrippa, strained to see up the stairway.

A door creaked open and a square of yellow sunlight stamped itself on the inky blackness below. Three Roman guards stood in the niche of light and began to descend toward the cells. A lighted fagot, held aloft by the man in the lead, revealed a roll of parchment in the hand of the second man. James tried not to look at the cold glimmer of a broadaxe as the flickering light fingered its way through the darkness.

The grim face of the jailer was pressed against the metal bars as the light, coming closer, gleamed against the brass chains of his breastplate. His eyes swept slowly over the miserable creatures on the floor within the dirty cell. Without a word, he thrust a key into the lock, and with a metallic scrape, rusty hinges protesting, the door swung open. Two of the soldiers made their way through the huddle of bodies, kicking and stepping on those who were not able to get out of the way. The jailer stumbled over an old man, crouched in half-sleep, seated near the apostle. With a loud curse, the soldier brought his weighted club down hard against the old man's head, releasing a flow of blood that ran quickly to the jaw and curled under the heavy, white beard. The wasted form of the elderly inmate crumpled in a lifeless heap at the feet of the soldier.

James, a prayer for courage in his heart, felt strong arms lifting him from the rancid floor. With senses reeling, he shuffled between the two burly soldiers toward the open door. The third man stood just outside the cell, reading in a monotone the proclamation for the execution of James, traitor to the Imperial Crown of Rome. As the soldier intoned the final words, he added as he rolled the parchment, "By order of his divine majesty, Herod Agrippa I."

. . . . .

Herod's unbridled lust for display had led him to order that the reception area adjacent to the throne room be inlaid with pure gold. Huge plaques of silver and rubies bedecked the magnificent room, already resplendent with costly tapestries from conquered lands. Vessels of gold and silver, marble statues, and ivory carvings that proclaimed the untold wealth of the mightiest empire the world had ever seen graced the palace. Placed conspicuously in the center of the long carpeted hallway which led to the king's quarters was a large marble bust of Caligula, assassinated emperor and close friend of Herod Agrippa.

Three priests from the Temple now sat without the throne room awaiting an audience with Herod. Perhaps their thoughts wandered back to Herod the Great, whose restoration of their beloved Temple was the one bright spot in the turbulent reign of that madman. The brutality of this mentally deranged king reached its apex in the mass slaughter of the infants in the city of Jerusalem, surpassing his murder of his firstborn son in a fit of rage.

In sharp contrast to that dark era of the rule of earlier Herods was the presence on the palace wall of an oversized Star of David. This symbol was placed there by Herod Agrippa himself to proclaim to the Jews that he was a true friend of the House of Israel. On the other hand, his hatred for Christians knew no bounds and he did everything in his power to crush the movement in his jurisdiction.

Despite his best efforts, Christian ranks were swelling, a fact that contributed to the unsettled state of his mind at this time. He, like the Herods before him, had a proclivity to mental imbalance. The recent execution of the Apostle James had merely served to spread the fires of "fanaticism" within the city.

At last, the great black and silver door to the throne room opened and a court herald summoned the priests to enter. Herod was seated upon his gilded throne, a crown of indescribable splendor adorning his head. A bejeweled scepter was lifted slightly in recognition of the visitors.

The chief priest approached the throne and said respectfully, "O mighty Herod, benefactor of the Jew and symbol of the power of Rome, give ear unto us, we pray." From the flattering lips of the priests, Herod learned that the execution of James was pleasing to the majority of the Jews, and that the political alliance between crown and Temple was secure.

Herod's eagerness to ingratiate himself with the leaders of Jewry was not to be confined merely to the death of James.

After the departure of the priests, he walked to the balustrade overlooking the sculptured lawns of the palace grounds. His gaze took in the great third wall that he had commanded to be built to the north of the city. As he stood in contemplation of his own greatness, his sister Herodias, wife of the banished Herod Antipas, came to stand beside him. She slipped her hand into his and urged Herod to sit with her.

"I have news for you, my brother!" purred Herodias. Herod distrusted his sister. She had succeeded in her evil ambition to silence John the Baptist in death only months earlier—a useless death, and completely unnecessary, thought Herod to himself. She had nearly equaled that success in her plan to discredit Herod Agrippa himself, though he was her own brother. This plan had failed, however, and issued only in the eventual banishment of Herod Antipas, her husband. It was with no little caution that Herod now listened to his sister.

"The man called Peter is back," she began. "He has let it be known that you arranged for James to be put to death. This could prove to be politically unsafe for you, Herod. With such a man moving freely about, your crown sits less easily upon your head, dear brother!"

Reaching for a fresh pomegranate, Herod let his gaze stray absently over the city below, shimmering in the heat.

"What would you have me do, Herodias, put him to the sword, also?" drawled Herod, arching an eyebrow. "He is, after all, a very important man among the filthy Christians."

"Only imprison him for a time, and I swear to you that these Christian vermin will fade away as the morning mist before the sun. They will then have no leader and their foolish beliefs will take wings. This I promise, my brother. For me, for Herodias, will you do this thing?" she cajoled.

For a long time Herod sat silent. Suddenly standing to his

feet, he looked down at his sister and held out his hand for her to kiss the Imperial ring.

"It shall be done. I must attend to the details." In an instant, Herod had crossed the shining marble floor and disappeared down a narrow corridor.

Herodias still sat in the reclining ivory chair which was covered with a deep scarlet velvet. She plucked a wild grape from the mountain of fruits on a silver platter, peeling it slowly as a smile of triumph crept across her face.

. . . . .

Young John Mark cautiously approached the two men standing in the cattle market. Evening was fast coming on and business was drawing to a close for the day. The men, intent on their proposed purchase of a young cow, failed to notice the entrance of the young man as he stationed himself nearby and leaned on the cattle guard. He noticed a long stick propped against the fence, and took it as he sat down upon a smooth rock a few feet distant. Inconspicuously, he began to draw lines upon the soft earth with the stick.

As the two men turned to leave, one of them chanced to look at the young man and recognized him as one of their number. His eyes guided those of his companion toward the ground. There, in a circle, John Mark had drawn the outline of a fish, symbol of the unpopular Christian movement.

Without drawing attention to themselves, the men sat quietly beside John on the large rock.

"What news have you?" asked one of them.

"Peter has been taken by Herod!" whispered the young man desperately.

The second man, pretending to fasten the latchet of his sandal, said, "Is he in prison yet?"

"He was being charged when I last saw him, but by now he is surely in chains!" replied John.

Standing, the first man said decisively, "We must go and inform the others. Tonight we meet at the home of Mary for prayer."

. . . . .

The apostle Peter, his ponderous frame held rigid as he gripped the long staff he carried, stood defiantly among the soldiers in the paved courtyard. This was the place of judgment, the very spot where the Christ had stood condemned before Herod the Great.

"Give place! Give place! Make way for the king!" rang out the order from the commander of the praetorian guard. A sharp flare of silver trumpets slashed through humid air, announcing the arrival of the king of Judea. Herod, swathed in a luxurious ermine robe, beneath which he wore a fresh pale blue linen vesture, ascended the seat of judgment. He looked at the impressive figure beneath him.

Herod, at thirty-four, was much younger than the apostle, whose age had begun to show in the silver streaks in his hair and beard. Herod felt admiration for this raucous fisherman, in spite of himself. This emotion gripped him momentarily now.

"What are the charges that are brought against this man?" demanded Herod, in his most impressive tone.

A representative of the chief priest stepped forward and was recognized.

"This man, known as Peter, has from time to time set forth strange doctrines which defy the religion of our fathers," he began. "It is commonly known that he has spoken not only against the God of Israel but against the king and the Emperor himself!"

Herodias had seated herself next to Herod on the judgment seat, and she now leaned forward to relish every moment of her triumph.

"What have you to say for yourself, Christian?" Herod demanded in icy tones.

Peter raised his hands held tightly together by a brass clamp tethered to a long chain which wound in serpentine fashion at his feet.

"The doctrine which I teach is not mine, nor is it strange! I do not pervert the religion of the Jews, but simply proclaim the gospel of the risen Christ, Lord of Herod and King of all the earth!" shouted Peter.

"You dare mention my name with that of a common peasant?" screamed Herod, his face purple with rage.

"One day you and all the rulers of the earth shall stand before the King of kings and be judged of him!" declared Peter as a steel-tipped lash bit deep into the flesh of his broad shoulders.

"I have heard enough! I will not be blasphemed by rabble!" thundered Herod. "Take him away! Put him in chains! Silence him!"

Herodias, fearful that Herod in his anger might give the order for Peter's immediate execution, intervened. Her designs did not include so sudden a loss of her opportunity to wreak vengeance upon the whole Christian community.

"My brother," she said softly, "let him be put in chains, yes, but let us make a public spectacle of this man to serve as a warning to the others. Do not put him to death, not yet. The people will see to that, later."

"What else can I do, Herodias? He has blasphemed me in public," whimpered the king.

Herodias pressed her point as she whispered, "It is near the time when Christians pay special homage to their king. Keep him in chains and bring him forth then to be judged before all the people. What more fitting way to teach these Christians to honor their king than to have their leader flogged and condemned on their most holy day?" she said, smiling wickedly.

"True! You do have my honor at heart, Herodias. Such loyalty shall not go unrewarded," concluded Herod.

Turning to face Peter, who still regarded him from below, Herod raised his hand and gave the order for the fisherman's removal. A Roman quaternion was detailed to escort Peter to the prison.

"Sixteen of my finest soldiers should be sufficient to see that this Christian behaves himself!" gloated Herod.

Herodias' eyes danced as she pressed her hand into her brother's and beamed contentedly at the ruler of the Jews.

. . . . .

"Go to sleep, Christian! Sing no more hymns or you will feel the bite of my lash again!" threatened the captain of the guard as he made his final round of inspection for the night.

Peter was securely shackled between two of the largest soldiers in the company.

All three sat down on the dirty straw-covered floor of the cell. With many grunts and complaints about their surroundings and the extra precautions taken with their prisoner, the guards settled down amid the squalor and tried to rest their heads against the stone wall.

Soon sleep overtook the guards and their famous prisoner. Two additional soldiers stood at attention at the cell door. Peter slept fitfully, twisting his bruised wrists beneath the brass fetters. His bleeding back, criss-crossed with the stripes he had received before being pushed into the cell, quivered spasmodically in response to pure pain.

Gradually, amid snores from the guards who were chained with Peter and those of several prisoners along the cell block, the entire prison area began to grow brighter with a strange, unearthly illumination. The sentries at the cell door looked at each other, eyes widening in stark terror as the brightness changed to dazzling glory. They were immobilized before the overpowering figure of an angel of God. He moved his hand and the very air seemed to tremble at his might.

The prison was aglow as the angelic being touched the door of the cell where Peter slept. The door swung wide and he walked over to Peter, sleeping between the two guards. The soldiers awoke and stared in frozen awe at the heavenly messenger. The angel touched Peter on his side and awakened him. The apostle, thinking he was dreaming, looked up at the glorious personage before him and smiled.

"Arise, Peter, and go quickly!" commanded the angel as he touched the shackles that bound Peter to his captors, causing them to clatter to the floor.

"Put your sandals on your feet and your garment about you, and follow me," he directed.

As they moved down the long corridor, the prison was lighted by the radiance that shone from the angel, revealing the huddled masses of prisoners, some sleeping, some now awake and staring in wonder at the scene before them.

Suddenly, the door which led to the officers' quarters opened and a centurion entered the cell area. As he locked the door and turned about, he fell back against the wall, eyes aghast, as he beheld Peter and the angel walking toward him.

The locked door opened wide as the angel pointed at it, and Peter stepped through into the outer guard precinct. The prison was constructed in a maze of wards or sections, and Peter had been confined in the third ward from the main gate.

Passing the first two wards safely, they came at last to the huge iron gate which led into the street and freedom. Peter was no longer surprised to see the massive door swing open of its own accord.

As they traveled down the narrow darkened street

outside the walls of the prison, the heavenly being suddenly took leave of Peter, leaving him standing in astonishment, as though he had awakened from a dream. Peter pressed his face into his hands and stood motionless on the cobblestones. In his heart, he knew that this had been no dream or vision and that God had surely heard his prayer for deliverance. He knew, too, of the Roman patrols that ranged through the city. Walking quickly in the shadows of buildings and down dark alleyways, he made his way toward the edge of the city and freedom.

. . . . .

Rhoda was a young Christian, both in years and in commitment to Christ. She had heard only the day before of the love of God and had embraced the faith.

Fervent prayers arose from the Christians assembled at the home of Mary as they petitioned God for Peter's deliverance from prison.

Suddenly Rhoda raised her head sharply, thinking she had heard a rapping on the outer gate. Her heart leaped as she envisioned brutal Roman soldiers demanding entrance. Not wishing to disturb the others who were in prayer, she moved in dreaded anticipation of what she might find as the knocking became louder and more insistent. Summoning her last ounce of courage, she slid the small iron bar away from the aperture in the gate. The sight that greeted her was almost beyond her comprehension. The man who stood at the gate was Peter himself! With unbounded joy, she slid the bar back in place and stood trembling. Her emotions were so wild in that moment that she turned and fled toward the house to inform the others.

Rushing back into the closeted room where daily prayer was held, she almost shouted, "Peter is here! He is here!"

Several of the women, thinking Rhoda was under severe strain, grouped themselves about her to console her.

"No! No! You don't understand! Peter is standing at the gate this very moment!" she exclaimed.

"Child," soothed Miletus, an elderly man who had known Rhoda all her life, "you are ill. Go lie down while we continue in prayer."

"I tell you, he is here in answer to our prayers! That is Peter knocking!"

"She is mad!" exclaimed a young man from the corner of the room.

Now the knocking became so loud that they all heard it. The same young man, putting his hand over his mouth in astonishment said, "We are all mad. We must be!"

Rushing to the gate, the group stopped short.

"Perhaps it is his angel! Herod must already have put him to death!" wailed a woman softly.

Rhoda pushed her way to the gate and opened it, revealing the figure of Peter. The astonished disciples led him into the house where he related all that had happened to him since his arrest.

Prayers of gratitude rose from hearts now charged with new faith as the gate was secured and the silent night deepened over Jerusalem.

. . . . .

"Dare you stand there and tell me that he left your charge in the middle of the night in the company of an angel? Do you take me for a fool?" Herod was screaming. He had rushed to the prison when awakened in his quarters and told that Peter had escaped. He was furious as he stood glaring at the captain of the guard.

"My men are still searching for him, Sire. He won't get far, I promise you," said the captain, visibly shaken.

"I want no promises, I want that prisoner! Now!"

"But, Sire . . ." stammered the bewildered captain, as he

held his hands before him in a gesture of helplessness. The two guards who had been shackled with Peter stood next to their commander, manacles still dangling from their wrists.

Herod turned and gave an order to the palace guards.

"Take them!" he commanded. The guards closed ranks about the three condemned men. His eyes smoldering with rage, Herod shouted at them, "You die for this, you fools!"

With that, the king stalked out of the cell block, his curses reverberating the length of the stone corridor.

. . . . .

Herod sat upon his throne in Caesarea where he had repaired to confer with delegates from the Phoenician cities of Tyre and Sidon.

Before him were gathered two hundred officials and delegates from the twin cities as they prepared to hear a speech by the renowned king of Judea.

Herod, an accomplished orator, took much delight in his ability to turn a phrase and to play upon the emotions of his audience. Indeed, this assembly was as captivated by his eloquence as many had been in the past. They punctuated his oration from time to time with shouts of "This is not the voice of a man but of a god!" "Herod is not a man! Only the gods have such power in speech!" This display of appreciation was not unmixed with flattery, but Herod savored it as though it were a rare dish set before him.

Without warning, excruciating pain slammed through his body and the great Herod gasped. His eyes bulging, he clutched his vesture and fell heavily to the floor.

As the lifeless form of Herod Agrippa I lay crumpled before his throne, the slimy, whitish creatures that crept from his eyes, his nose, his ears, and swarmed across his face belied the permanence and incorruptibility of his kingdom.

Black Magic and Blue Tapestry

Based on Acts 13:6-11

Legendary Mount Olympus, rising six thousand feet above the island of Cyprus in the Mediterranean Sea, looked placidly down upon the village of Paphos. The Spirit of the risen Christ had spoken to Barnabas and Paul, men destined to take the gospel to the Gentiles. In Antioch, the city where first the disciples were labeled with the derisive title of "Christian," the command was given to move out with the good news of salvation to all men. Hands had been laid upon these men and the Holy Spirit constrained them to forsake all else and go to a hostile world with the message of a living Savior. Cyprus lay directly in their path.

Barnabas, himself a native of Salamis on the eastern coast of the island, was familiar with the traditions of his people and the resistance with which any attempt to introduce the message of Jesus Christ would be met. The island was steeped in superstition and legends of the gods, not the least of which was veneration of Aphrodite, goddess of fertility.

Paul, upon hearing these things from his companion, planned his strategy. On the ship he had knelt with Barnabas and John Mark to seek the guidance and the protection of the Lord Jesus, believing prayer to be the first line of defense against the paganism they would shortly encounter.

In the misty distance, they could make out the commanding heights of Mount Olympus, mythical home of the gods whose father was Zeus. As the ship drew near the rocky island set like a sun-drenched jewel in the glistening Mediterranean, blue-walled houses capped with bright red tile roofs greeted their eyes. The greenery of lush vineyards patterned the jagged hillsides as flocks of fat sheep grazed contentedly in the warmth of the sun.

The arrival of the Christians on Cyprus did not go unnoticed. Roman legions swarmed the entire island, strategic center of the Empire's eastern dominions since Cyprus had come under the military yoke of Rome. The village of Paphos took no little pride in its importance as the site of a huge temple dedicated to the worship of Aphrodite.

It was to this temple that a villager had retreated with the news of the arrival of the apostle and his companions. There, in the very center of the tile floor of the temple's holy of holies, rose a gigantic stone in the shape of a cone without a point. This blunt monument served the local patrons as a "statue" to the goddess in lieu of a more lifelike figurine.

Temple priests invoked the blessings of Aphrodite amid the incense-filled sanctuary. A young man, clad in the vesture of a woman, approached the stone, imitating the voice of a woman as he chanted an ancient song to the goddess of all life. He then made sacrifice of a young dove, sprinkling the warm blood over the sacred stone. These pagan rites were performed in preparation for the encounter with the missionaries who bore a strange and unwelcome message to their island.

It became immediately apparent to the Christians that they had happened upon Paphos in the midst of a swirling, boisterous celebration. Large oxen lumbered through the narrow cobblestone streets lugging wooden carts laden with freshly cut flowers. Young girls, singing and dancing, surrounded the carts scattering flowers before the priests, who made their way through the center of the village.

"These are celebrating the annual flower festival, and it has just begun," explained Barnabas to the bewildered Paul. "Drunken orgies will follow the parade, in the temple of Aphrodite. These poor people believe that the goddess can increase the yield of their crops and bless their families."

Paul watched as cart after cart, loaded with fragrant blossoms, rumbled past. His heart went out to the people of the village as he beheld the paganism to which they had so freely given themselves.

"Jesus Christ can show to them a more excellent way of life. We are here to lift him up among men such as these," mused the apostle as he and Barnabas waited to cross the narrow street.

. . . . .

Sergius Paulus, Roman governor of Cyprus under Caesar Augustus, was a man of considerable learning. He had first heard of the existence of the religion which had taken its name from the peasant carpenter of Nazareth when he was allowed to examine official reports of the trial and execution of Jesus. He was held in high regard by the Emperor—a fact which, combined with some political pressure from his friends in Rome, had assured his appointment to Paphos as proconsul. He had assumed his duties with such dispatch and efficiency that he quickly ennobled himself in the sight of Caesar.

He tolerated the fawning of political and religious figures of the province, not the least of whom was Elymas, turncoat Jew and "prophet." Elymas had acquired his position with Sergius Paulus on the pretext of his ability to foretell events, both military and political, some of which had actually come to pass. The governor had been impressed, quite as much with this man's facility in fortune-telling as with his religious ardor. Elymas, whose Jewish name was Bar-jesus, was a devotee of Aphrodite and was instrumental in persuading the Emperor himself to accept many of Sergius Paulus' proposals, thus creating for himself a comfortable niche on the governor's staff.

The message concerning the presence of the disciples on the island prompted an immediate reaction on the part of Elymas. Making his way to the Roman ruler's quarters, he concocted several stories which were designed to turn Sergius Paulus against the missionaries at the outset.

Walking quickly toward the brass door which led to the governor's chambers, Elymas was accosted by two Roman guards who apparently did not know him, having been ordered there with a fresh military contingent only the previous week, to bolster Rome's hold on the Mediterranean.

"Your name!" snapped one of the soldiers.

"Tell the governor that Elymas wishes to speak with him," replied the crafty Bar-jesus.

"Stay," ordered the other, shoving his shield forward toward Elymas. The other guard entered the governor's quarters in brisk military fashion. He quickly reappeared and said, "Enter, Elymas. The governor will see you now."

The sorcerer gave the guards a frown of disapproval as he sidled past them and entered the presence of the most powerful man in Cyprus.

A powder blue tapestry etched in pure gold braid hung above the governor's chair. The calculating mind of Elymas quickly reasoned its value and he cast about for some scheme whereby he might obtain the beautiful fabric for himself.

He shelved the idea for the present as he approached the person of Sergius Paulus, proconsul of the Empire of Rome.

The governor had been examining a report of military installations on the island and did not look up as Elymas seated himself. Through the months of association with

Sergius, Elymas had become familiar with military courtesy and remained silent until the governor completed his report and rolled up the parchment.

Glancing up, Sergius said in a congenial tone, "Elymas, my friend, welcome. How go things with you today?"

Always the diplomat, Elymas replied, "Quite well, my lord, but only because of the efficiency and benevolence of our governor!"

Sergius Paulus smiled appreciatively as he poured rich red wine into two crystal tumblers.

"From the Eternal City itself!" he observed as he savored the heady aroma. "It came along on the troopship. A gift from the Emperor!" he concluded, handing the sparkling liquid to Elymas.

"What news have you, my friend?" pressed the governor. "Surely you do not wish me again to request more funds for your temple?" he said querulously.

"No, my lord," replied Elymas, "the generous gift to Aphrodite the governor made last month will suffice for many years."

"What then? Would you have me don a festive costume and join that procession of drunken revelers on the streets?" Sergius asked, laughing.

Becoming serious, Elymas leaned forward in his seat. "Your Eminence, there is on this island this very moment one who could destroy everything political and religious that we have both worked so hard for. He is a dangerous man and should be dealt with accordingly."

"Speak up, man! Who is on the island? Who is dangerous?" demanded the proconsul.

"He defiles the noble Roman name of Paulus. He is called a Christian, after the despicable religion begun in Jerusalem by the carpenter, Jesus of Nazareth. Christians believe that their founder rose from the tomb after crucifixion and lives again. Foolishness! Foolishness!" exclaimed Elymas, shaking his head.

"Paulus? He is a Roman citizen?" queried Sergius.

"Yes, my lord. He is a Jew like myself, but a Roman citizen by right of birth, having been born in Tarsus of Cilicia. Never has a more dangerous man come through the Cilician Gates. Hear him not, Sergius Paulus, I implore you in the sacred name of Aphrodite," urged Elymas.

"I have heard of a man named Paul," mused the governor, pouring himself another drink. "This man was called Saul until he met with a most interesting experience on the highway to Damascus, so the story goes. Is that the man of whom you speak?" asked Sergius, who was not in the habit of accepting false answers.

"Yes. It is the same man. He has caused nothing but turmoil wherever he has gone. His religion serves no other purpose than to divide men in their ancient allegiance to the true gods," Elymas replied. He sat, empty glass gripped tightly, as he spoke the warning which he hoped would be heeded by the Roman.

"If I recall correctly, this Paul has been associated with a fisherman named Simon who was imprisoned by Herod Agrippa. You remember, Elymas, what a miserable death Herod suffered at Caesarea of Philippi." Sergius rose, walked over to the stone fireplace, and stood staring into the ashes. "Perhaps, Elymas, it was because Herod would not listen to this man Simon that he met such a sorry fate," he said after some time, more to himself than to Elymas. Turning the tumbler in his hand as he studied it intently, Sergius announced slowly and decisively, "I will see him, Elymas. I will see this dangerous man called Paul."

Jumping to his feet, Elymas almost shouted, "See him, hear him, and you will surely call the wrath of Aphrodite down upon you, Sergius Paulus!"

"I have spoken, Elymas! You are dismissed!" exclaimed the Roman, eyes blazing at this impertinence.

Elymas moved toward the door. He knocked twice as a signal, then turned again to Sergius Paulus. "Paul is spreading vicious lies, Sergius," he snapped. "I warn you now—the responsibility is all yours if you hear him!"

The guard held the door as Elymas stalked out, making his way toward the sounds of revelry on the street below.

. . . . .

As the Cyprian night closed about him, Elymas sat brooding in the Temple of Aphrodite. He consulted his books on the ancient arts of black magic and astrology. Before him were flasks containing various liquids, some of which foamed and swirled in a manner which suggested evil.

Surely, within these books there is a way to influence Sergius Paulus against the Christians, he thought.

Walking over to a large brazier which was kept burning at all times, he took a pinch of powder from a flask and cast it into the flames. Immediately the room was filled with an oppressive evil power. Elymas sank to the floor of the temple, eyes glassy and staring. He sat looking blankly into the licking flames as the trance wore on. From time to time he responded with a coarse laugh as though hearing some tremendous joke from the shades of another world.

As suddenly as it had begun, the trance ceased. Elymas put his hands to his face and swayed slowly from side to side, the brilliance of the fire reflected in the huge silver bracelets and rings which he wore.

"My answer! My answer! I have my answer!" he exclaimed.

The emptiness of the huge temple rang with the demonic laughter of Elymas as the leaping flames died to a shimmering mass of coals.

. . . . .

The next morning disclosed trampled flowers, empty carts, and wandering oxen upon the narrow cobblestone streets. This was the aftermath of the pagan Festival of Flowers. The streets were deserted and the Temple of Aphrodite closed against further demonstrations of worship.

Two figures approached the palace of the governor of Cyprus and slowly ascended the stone steps. Roman guards commanded the men to halt.

"Who goes there?" challenged the sentry.

"Paul and Barnabas, to see the governor," came the reply.

"Come," said the second soldier. "The governor waits to see you."

The disciples followed the Roman to the brass door upon which was emblazoned the official seal of Rome and the name, *Sergius Paulus, Governor,* set in shining brass beneath the eagle.

The Roman procurator stood as the men came toward his huge teakwood desk.

"Greetings, in the name of Jesus Christ," saluted Paul.

"I am delighted to see you," replied Sergius almost too eagerly. "Please sit down."

The governor took the hand of each of the men in the traditional Roman handclasp of friendship.

"I have long wished to meet you, Paul," said Sergius, seating himself. "I am familiar with your work among those of us you refer to as 'Gentiles.' I am curious to know more of this religion of yours."

"It is not mine but Christ's," said Paul simply. "He it is who works within us and manifests his power to heal and to save."

"Yes, I understand—I think. But tell me, does this religion not claim to have a founder who rose from the dead?

I have been engaged in many bloody conflicts for the honor of Rome, and I have seen many good men fall in death. Never have I seen one leave his grave! How can this be?"

Just as Paul was about to explain the meaning of the resurrection to the ruler, the door opened and Elymas entered, unannounced. He was obviously still laboring under the power of the trance he had conjured the night before. He weaved noticeably as he walked.

"Elymas! State your business and leave me, quickly!" exclaimed the irate governor.

"My lord, I am here on a mission of mercy," announced the crafty magician. "Indeed, I have come to deliver you from these men who would lead the glorious Sergius Paulus astray, to follow after their wild babblings!"

Elymas held out a long metal rod decorated with curious markings and pointed it at the floor before him. A huge black cloud erupted instantly, and on the floor slithered three glistening reptiles.

"Is the religion of Paul powerful enough to produce the likes of that?" exulted the sorcerer. "Or this?" Elymas pointed the rod at the blue tapestry which he had admired earlier.

From its place on the wall above the governor's chair, the beautiful fabric slid, collapsing on the floor in a heap.

"Ho, Sergius! Let us trade!" cried Elymas boisterously. "My vipers for your tapestry!"

The governor, wishing to be rid of the raucous intruder, shouted, "Take the tapestry for your temple, but get those creatures out of here!"

Elymas walked triumphantly toward the beautiful tapestry and held it tenderly as he glared at Paul and Barnabas. Pointing his divining rod at the snakes, he mumbled some unintelligible words, and the serpents were no more.

Waving the rod slowly in Paul's face, Elymas droned menacingly, "Christian, dare you come to the governor to tell him your fairy tale? He is too intelligent to believe the lies you teach!"

Turning to the procurator, Elymas said, "Sergius Paulus, can any rational man accept the story that a man can die and live again? Send these away. Do not listen to their fables. Look to Aphrodite, true spirit of all life! You have seen for yourself the power of the great goddess."

Paul rose from his chair, his face red with anger, and pointed at Elymas across the room.

"You child of the devil!" cried the apostle. "You stand in the way of all that is good and decent. You are full of the tricks of Satan, and by them you seek to twist the Lord's truth into lies! Behold, the hand of the living Christ is upon you, Elymas. Total blindness shall come upon you as punishment for your perverted and evil ways!"

Even as the magician stood sneering at Paul, he felt a numbness growing in his forehead. As his sight rapidly left him, he stumbled wildly about the room, falling headlong over objects until he collapsed near the door.

"Help me!" he cried in terror. "Please, somebody help me! I'm blind! O dear God of Israel, I am blind!"

Sergius Paulus summoned the guards who lifted Elymas to his feet. As they led the mumbling sorcerer out of the room, he clutched the blue tapestry to his breast and lifted his sightless eyes to the heavens.

Pagan Nightmare

Based on Acts 16:14-18

Built atop a steep, rugged hill, the Roman colony of Philippi commanded a magnificent view of the Aegean Sea and had rapidly become an important commercial center. The growing city enjoyed the reputation of being the site of the historic and decisive battle between the forces of Marc Antony and those of Brutus less than a century earlier, as well as being the first Gentile city to hear the gospel of the risen Christ.

Morning was breaking slowly over the sprawling city as two men emerged from the elaborately impressive home of Lydia. She had accepted the gospel only the day before, as she had listened to an inspired Apostle Paul speaking to a gathering of women beside the beautiful Gangites River. Her occupation as a seller of purple linen, manufactured in Macedonia and sold to men of wealth, had enabled her to purchase the lovely home overlooking the river. Now Paul and Silas, missionaries of the gospel to the Gentiles, had been invited to make her home their center of activity.

Silas closed the door softly to avoid awakening the household, and the two made their way eastward toward the river where several believers would be awaiting their instructions in the Way.

The city was awakening all around them as the missionaries strode toward their meeting place. Women were leaving their homes to go to the public fountain to draw water for the morning meal. The clean air of the sea wafted its way inland and fluttered the imperial pennant atop a bronze pole at the entrance to the barracks area. Julius Caesar had decreed that soldiers who had lost their lands while in military service should be quartered at public expense at Philippi. Many of the famed praetorian guard made their home here, also. Originally, the presence of the soldiers was occasioned by the existence of gold mines that lay to the west of the city. Greed had driven many of the citizens to lawlessness, and Caesar permanently stationed a detachment of soldiers at Philippi to oversee mining of the precious metal.

At the end of the narrow pavement which ran beside the military compound stood a huge bronze statue of the Roman soldier Gaius Vibius, noted for some forgotten battle. His visage was lifted skyward, with shield clutched in the left hand, while in the right a broad two-edged battle sword was lofted at a forward angle. Beneath his feet, encased in protective armor plating, lay the prostrate form of a vanquished soldier.

As Paul and Silas approached the war memorial, the morning sun revealed a young woman peering around the great marble base. She alternately poked her head above the base of the statue and disappeared from view. Suddenly, as Paul and Silas came abreast of the statue, she ran from behind the marble column and threw her arms upward to the sky, now streaked with splashes of red and gold. Sea gulls punctuated the lightened horizon, adding a wild note to the rigid figure silhouetted against the dawn. The breeze rose sharply, whipping her purple garment until it swirled madly about her body. She stood thus for a long moment, then with an unearthly shriek threw her arms to her sides, stiffened, and glared with hollow eyes at the men.

Silas looked questioningly at his companion as Paul laid his hand on Silas' arm in gentle restraint. They stopped and watched as the woman slowly raised her hand and pointed menacingly at them. With a wild toss of her head, the wind wrapping her long black hair about her face and neck, she screamed, "These men are servants of the most high God, which show unto us the way of salvation!" A nerve-shattering cackle resounded against the sea cliffs as she bowed in mock humility. Remaining in that position, she laughed uncontrollably, her frail body racked with the spasm of demonic seizure.

"Leave her," Paul said bluntly, taking Silas' arm and guiding him around the sobbing girl.

"But, Paul, look at her! Is there nothing we can do?" asked Silas, looking back at the pitiful figure.

"The Lord has a purpose in this, but now is not the appointed time," explained the apostle.

The two continued their journey to the riverside for the dawn prayer meeting.

. . . . .

An oracle to Diana of Ephesus had been in existence at Philippi since the arrival of King Philip of Macedon in 356 B.C., who named the city in honor of himself. It was believed that if the worshiper desired to learn of future events, he had only to come to the sacred oracle, or altar, and make his request known to the priestess. Hers was the privilege of interceding for the devoted follower of Diana and petitioning the goddess for the desired revelation.

The priestess stationed herself atop a circular slab of stone which rested on three huge legs. After the worshiper performed certain acts of purification, he was permitted to approach the priestess and make his petition. A vapor would then mysteriously issue from a cleft in the floor of the "holy place" and intoxicate the priestess, thus enabling her to receive a "revelation" from the goddess Diana. Upon awakening, the priestess would command a scribe to set down on parchment those things she supposedly had heard from the very lips of the goddess. The believer would be given the document containing the revelation and charged an exorbitant fee. Thus, the priestess contributed greatly to the wealth of her masters, the temple priests.

It was the custom to select the future priestess from among the local populace. She was, as a rule, a simple girl, easily persuaded to engage in such traffic. This had been the calling of Jeriel for nearly a year, since the day the temple priests had come to her home and informed her parents that the goddess had chosen their daughter for this signal honor. She had remained true to the code of Diana and did, indeed, appear to be possessed of a spirit of divination, or gift to discern the mysterious. Many of the townspeople and men of elevated rank in the Empire had gone to Jeriel for advice and revelations.

This unearthly power, however, had lately overcome her judgment, and she had startled even the temple priest with her frenzied interpretations of purported revelations from the goddess. So totally had she succumbed to the curious art that at times she was far removed from rational behavior. The latest such incident had occurred the day before, on the seventh day of the month, traditionally heralded as the birthday of Apollo. Engaged in the bizarre inspection of the entrails of a bird in an attempt to secure a revelation, she had suddenly overturned the sacrificial altar upon which lay the bloody creature, and had run screaming from the temple, "Great is Diana of the Ephesians! Give honor to Apollo! Hear the wisdom of Diana and worship Apollo!"

This outburst was good advertisement for her masters' craft, so she was not detained. Running wildly through the colony, she had collapsed near the statue of Gaius Vibius. There she had slept fitfully through the chilly night and had awakened to see Paul and Silas approaching her.

For three successive mornings, this experience repeated itself. The missionaries were growing accustomed to the ghostly specter of Jeriel in the gray mists. She screamed the same words at the men each time they passed the statue, which she had adopted as a temporary oracle. On this, the fourth morning, things took a different turn.

Jeriel stepped from behind the column and screamed above the wind, "These men are servants of the most high God, which show us the way of salvation!" This time, however, she did not bow to the missionaries, but stood her ground defiantly. With sheer fury smoldering in her dark eyes, she trembled visibly as Paul stepped closer.

"Touch me not, Christian!" she spat as Paul attempted to lay his hand on her shaking arm. She threw her priestly cape over her shoulder, revealing the serpent bracelet of Python, symbol of her holy office. Her nails were caked with filth, no doubt from much rummaging through ashy remains of sacrificed animals. Her face, once that of a lovely girl, was now distorted with the agony of the damned.

Suddenly, Paul thrust both arms forward, pinning her hands to her sides. She struggled furiously, trying to wrest herself from his grip. Though a small man, Paul was strong and well able to control her wild thrashing. Looking steadily at the tortured girl, he said in a voice echoing with authority, "I command thee in the name of Jesus Christ, come out of her!"

Instantly Jeriel's body ceased its uncontrollable tremors. As a cloud passing the face of the sun, the look of stark terror faded from her eyes, and the light of sanity returned.

Slowly, she relaxed her tensed arms and smiled, as through awakening from some terrible nightmare. Paul took her by the arm and turned her toward the sound of a hymn lifting from somewhere near the rising of the sun.